My Lords, Ladies and Gentlemen

My Lords, Ladies and Gentlemen

The best and funniest after-dinner stories
from the famous

Collected by
PHYLLIS
SCHINDLER

PIATKUS

This book has been compiled for two reasons: one, to help Guy's Hospital Paediatric Renal Unit to purchase badly needed equipment; the other, to amuse and inform the reader, potential after-dinner speaker and, of course, his audience.

My most grateful thanks to the eminent contributors and especially to the Rt. Hon. Lord Denning, who has allowed his name to be associated with the worthy cause.

First published in
Great Britain in 1986 by
Piatkus Books Ltd of
5 Windmill Street, London W1T 2JA
info@piatkus.co.uk

Reprinted 23 times

This edition published 2004

Reprinted 2006

The moral rights of the author have been asserted

A catalogue record for this book is available from the British Library

ISBN 0–7499–2538–8

Phototypeset in 11/13pt Linotron Palatino by
Phoenix Photosetting, Chatham
Printed and bound in Great Britain by
Biddles Ltd, King's Lynn, Norfolk

Contributors

Foreword by Lord Denning 9

Larry Adler 11
Lord Jeffrey Archer 12
John Arlott 13
David Atterton 14
Richard Baker 16
K. A. Ballard 17
Professor David Bellamy 17
Lord Brabazon of
Tara 18
Lord Brabourne 19
Sir Alastair Burnet 20
Peter Cadbury 21
Victor Canning 23
Dame Barabara Cartland 24
The Rt. Hon. The Lord
Chalfont 25
Shirley Conran 25
The Rt. Hon. Sir W. Allan
Davis 26
Dame Judi Dench 26
The Rt. Hon. Lord
Denning 27
Anthony Denny 28
Anne Diamond 29
The Rt. Hon. Sir John
Donaldson 30
Dame Mary Donaldson 30
Paul Eddington 31
The Rt. Rev. and Rt. Hon.
Gerald Ellison 32
The Rt. Hon. Lord
Elwyn-Jones 33
Sir Monty Finniston 34

The Rt. Hon. The Earl
Fortescue 35
Christina Foyle 36
John Francome 37
W. B. Fraser 39
Sir David Frost 40
Sir Peter Gadsden 41
Sir Ronald Gardner-
Thorpe 42
His Honour Judge
Goldstone 43
The Rt. Hon. Lord
Goodman 44
Alderman
M. A. Graham 45
Jimmy Greaves 46
Sir Desmond Heap 47
Rachael Heyhoe Flint 48
Michael Hill 49
Admiral of the Fleet
The Lord Hill-Norton 50
The Rt. Hon. Baron Home
of The Hirsel 51
Anthony Hopkins 52
Sir Edward Howard 53
Sir David Hunt 54
The Rt. Hon. Douglas
Hurd 55
Rufus Ide 56
Jayne Irving 58
The Very Reverend
Lawrence Jackson 59
David Jacobs 61
P. D. James 62

Alderman Brian Jenkins 63

Sir Anthony Jolliffe 64

John Junkin 66

Henry Kelly 67

Ludovic Kennedy 68

His Honour Alan
King-Hamilton 68

The Rev. Dr. B. A. C.
Kirk-Duncan 69

The Hon. Sir John Latey 70

A 'Lawyer Friend' 71

Another 'Lawyer Friend' 72

Sir Christopher Leaver 74

The Rt. Hon. Lord
Mancroft 75

The Rt. Hon. The Lord
Marsh 76

Alderman Clive Martin 77

Christopher Martin-
Jenkins 78

Julia McKenzie 79

Norris D. McWhirter 80

Alderman Francis
McWilliams 81

Cliff Michelmore 82

George Mikes 83

Sir John Mills 85

John Minchall-Fogg 86

Sir Patrick Moore 87

Stirling Moss 88

Cyril Murkin 89

The Rt. Hon. Sir Patrick
Nairne 89

Sir David Napley 90

J. E. Neary 91

His Honour Judge
Aron Owen 89

Sir Peter Parker 94

John F. Phillips 95

His Honour Judge Pigot 96

Lady Porter 97

Dr. J. M. Rae 99

His Honour Judge
Ranking 100

Frederic Raphael 101

Sir Lindsay Ring 103

Rt. Hon. Lord Robens 104

Robert Robinson 104

Jean Rook 105

Alderman David Rowe-
Ham 106

G. W. Rowley 106

Norman Royce 107

Sir Percy Rugg 108

Sheila Scott 110

Sir Harry Secombe 110

The Rt. Hon. The Earl of
Selkirk 111

'Someone in the City' 111

His Honour Judge John
Slack 112

Colonel, Alderman Greville
Spratt 113

Oliver Sunderland 114

Jimmy Tarbuck 115

His Honour Judge Anthony
Tibber 116

The Rt. Hon. Viscount
Tonypandy 116

Sir Alan Traill 117

The Rt. Hon. Lord
Tweedsmuir 118

Terry Waite 119

Ian Wallace 120

Irving Wallace 121

The Rev. Basil Watson 122

Katharine Whitehorn *123*
Lord Wigoder *124*
Dorian Williams *124*
Emlyn Williams *125*

Sir Max Williams *126*
Lord Willis of
Chislehurst *127*
Sir Hugh Wontner *128*

Foreword
by Rt. Hon. Lord Denning P.C., D.L.
Master of the Rolls 1962–1982

The title to a book should be striking and descriptive. This title, *My Lords, Ladies and Gentlemen,* is both. It brings to mind at once great banquets at Guildhall or Mansion House, and splendid dinners at the Savoy or Claridges – attended by the men with their stiff shirts, white ties, decorations and medals, and by the ladies in their lovely dresses sparkling with diamonds and jewels. The speeches, to be a success, should be short and simple, light and serious, witty and entertaining – all mixed together to delight the hearers. Above all, they should be well spoken, clearly and distinctly, not too fast or yet too slow, with the occasional pause for effect. How few speakers come up to that standard!

Mrs. Phyllis Shindler (the wife of Alfred Shindler, Chairman of the Establishment Committee of the City of London) has chosen the title, *My Lords, Ladies and Gentlemen,* as a lead into a selection of the very best after-dinner stories – as told by the authors and repeated by the plagiarists. I am afraid that very few of such stories are original. A speaker hits upon one, usually a phrase with a *double entendre.* It goes down well: so well that it is repeated in the next few weeks or months or years – always without acknowledgment of its source – always to the groans of those habitués who have heard it already several times before.

I am much impressed by the list of names who have contributed to the book. They are among the most distinguished of our time and have themselves attended the best dinners, made the best speeches and listened to the best stories. They come from the Arts, the City of London, the Church, Industry, Sport, the Law, the Lords themselves, and from past Lord Mayors of London (sometimes called 'late' Lord Mayors). Speaking of Lords, perhaps I may add a nice story first told by my good friend the late Cyril Asquith (Lord Asquith of Bishopstone). He said that the ideal judge at first instance was one who was 'short, simple and wrong'. But that, he added, was not to say that the province of the Court of Appeal was to be 'long, tedious and right' because that would be to usurp the prerogative of the House of Lords!

The reason for this unique collection is the best of reasons. It is to help the best of causes at the best of hospitals, namely, Guy's. I am myself ever grateful for the care the doctors and nurses there took of my first wife during weeks of illness – and, when she recovered, where my son was born. This book is published especially to aid the Paediatric Renal Unit of Guy's Hospital. Shorn of medical jargon, that means the department of Guy's which treats children suffering from kidney trouble. It is the largest in the United Kingdom and the second largest in Europe. It accepts many children suffering from kidney disorders and saves their lives. It also does a great deal of research into the causes and treatment of kidney disorders.

The proceeds from the sale will be devoted to the purchase of equipment. I do hope you will help by buying the book and thus do your part in expressing gratitude to Mrs. Shindler for her splendid effort on behalf of the Unit – all done entirely voluntarily for the good of the cause.

Jenkins

Larry Adler

Musician, Journalist, Writer and Composer

A man comes home, finds his wife in bed with his best friend. He goes to the bed, says to his friend, 'I *have* to . . . but *you*?'

Lord Jeffrey Archer
Author

An EEC delegation was drafted to discover what the significance would be of a Member of the Community going to either Heaven or Hell.

A parliamentary Group was selected and first went to Heaven and then reported back to Brussels thus:

The Germans were architects

The French were cooks

The Italians were lovers

The British were policemen and

The Swiss were politicians

The Group were then sent to Hell and came back to report that:

The Germans were police

The French were architects

The Italians were politicians

The British were cooks and

The Swiss were lovers.

John Arlott

O.B.E.

Writer and Broadcaster

The senior Soviet agent with responsibility for Britain came here to visit his contacts. Reaching the home town of his chief Welsh operative, he asked a man in the street, can you tell me where Mister Jones lives?

'We have a lot of Joneses here you know – what is his Christian name?' 'David'.

'We have a lot of David Joneses, too; is it

'Jones the post you want?'   'No'
'Jones the boot?'   'No'
'Jones the meat?'   'No'
'Jones the paint?'   'No'
'Jones the bus?'   'No'

'What does he do then?' 'He is the chairman of the local temperance society, chairman of the Conservative association, major of the territorials and master of foxhounds . . .'

'Oh, yes, of course, you mean Jones the Spy.'

David Atterton

C.B.E., Ph.D., F.Eng.

Industrialist

(This story can benefit from an Australian accent.) I remember being in Australia on a trip many years ago, before satellite communication, which necessitated telephoning England, the most convenient time being about 5.00 a.m. local Australian time. A bad line necessitated shouting and, when later I left my room, my friendly Australian neighbour said 'Good on you Pom, but why not let the phone do the work rather than shout all the way to England?'

The next morning, having to make another call, and with my neighbour in mind, I crept under the bedclothes with a torch, pencil, notebook and telephone; the call lasted some 25 minutes and, when I surfaced, the waiter most considerately had not only brought my breakfast in response to one of those cards hung on the door but had also brought a spare pot of coffee and another cup and saucer.

*   *   *

Speaking to you tonight reminds me of the American Professor of Nuclear Physics, who, as well as his duties as a Departmental Head, undertook a wide series of visiting lectures. Being driven one afternoon by his chauffeur to a lecture engagement at a University, a conversation developed when the chauffeur commented upon the unfairness of life; he was paid a paltry x thousand dollars per annum, whereas the Professor no doubt received a large salary and substantial sums for his lecture engagements. When the Professor mentioned that this was a reflection of their relative abilities, the chauffeur politely remonstrated 'Rubbish – he had sat at the back of the hall, heard this, and many other lectures such that he could do it without problem, particularly with the aid of slides'. 'Stop the car,' said the Professor, 'let us change places and you can give this evening's lecture'.

They were duly received by the Dean of the University and the chauffeur gave a splendid lecture with many gestures and learned quips, such that he received a standing ovation.

In his vote of thanks the Dean of the Faculty mentioned that he had assembled many of his most able research workers anxious to ask questions, and the chauffeur agreed, after a moment's hesitation. A most earnest young man asked 'What were the Professor's views on the structure of the negative proton?' Taken aback, the chauffeur paused, and replied slowly 'This is a most elementary, dare I say even a naïve question: it is in fact so simple that I will ask my chauffeur sitting in the back of the hall to answer it.'

Richard Baker

O.B.E., R.D.

Broadcaster and Author

One of my stories concerns an unfortunate lack of communication during a TV Outside Broadcast for the BBC. One of the essentials of this game is that the commentator and the camera director should have almost telepathic understanding, so that the commentary matches the shot on the screen and vice versa.

Some years ago I went on a Royal Tour of South America, and in the course of this the Queen visited the Chilean capital, Santiago. There she had to lay a wreath at the statue of one of Chile's great heroes, one Bernardo O'Higgins. We were televising the ceremony live via the satellite. The Director was a Chilean with almost no English, and he obviously had some difficulty in following what I was saying. The band came along playing 'Colonel Bogey' and I remarked that it sounded rather good on a band like this, complete with sousaphone.

'And by the way', I added, 'the sousaphone is that peculiar object you see sticking up in the middle of your picture now'. Alas, halfway through this sentence the director decided to cut to a close-up of the Duke of Edinburgh. Probably my most embarrassing moment among many during a long career in broadcasting.

K. A. Ballard
M.C., C.C.
Past Sheriff of the City of London, 1978

'Behind every successful man is an astonished mother-in-law!'

Professor David Bellamy
B.Sc., Ph.D., F.L.S., F.I.Biol
Botanist, Writer and Broadcaster

Did you hear the story about the two caterpillars crawling along a twig when a butterfly flew overhead? One caterpillar said to the other, 'You will never get me up in one of those things.'

*   *   *

Have you heard about the Irish jellyfish? IT SET!

Lord Brabazon of Tara
C.B.E.

A young man who had recently inherited a small fortune had heard about the advances in modern transplant surgery, and decided he would benefit from a new brain. He went to see a specialist and asked him what he could offer.

'Well', said the specialist, 'that depends on what you can afford. At the moment we have several brains in stock: that of a bank-clerk for £5,000, a University professor for £10,000 or a High Court judge for £20,000.'

'I am a wealthy man', said the young man. 'Tell me, what is your absolute best and most expensive one at the moment?'

'You are in luck', said the specialist, 'we happen to have a stockbroker's,* a very special offer at £50,000.'

'I don't understand', said the young man, 'why is a stockbroker's brain so much more expensive than any of the others?'

'Simple, it's hardly ever used', said the specialist.

* The last suggestion can be altered to suit the audience.

Lord Brabourne
Film and Television Producer

At lunch one day our family were discussing the problems of famine in Africa and elsewhere. It was mentioned that one of the main causes was over-population of the world.

After lunch, the younger members of the family continued the discussion and one of our seven-year-old twin sons, who had been looking very thoughtful, said, 'Is it really all to do with over-copulation?'!

Sir Alastair Burnet
Broadcaster

An American congressional candidate was running
behind in the polls so his campaign manager told him:
'There's an Indian reservation up the road. You might
just pick up some votes if you made them a few
promises.'

The Indian chief was pleased by the attention and
called his people to listen. The politician began: 'Vote for
me and I promise you hot and cold running water
throughout your reservation.'

The audience murmured 'Goomwah.'

The politician's hopes rose: 'Vote for me and I promise
you a paved road all the way to Tucson.'

The audience shouted: 'Goomwah! Goomwah!'

The politician, much encouraged, went still further:
'Vote for me and I promise you cable television in your
village.'

The audience shouted: 'Goomwah! Goomwah!
Goomwah!'

The politician was delighted, and all the more when the
chief took him down to the corral and presented him with
a pony.

'We never heard anything like that before,' said the
chief politely. 'Now mind you don't step in any of the
goomwah.'

Peter Cadbury

Chairman of the George Cadbury Trust 1979 to present

When I was practising at the Bar I was asked to defend a man who was charged with 'being in possession of an illicit still'. His defence was that he had not used it, although he had it in his possession. I persuaded him that he had no defence, so he said 'I would like a number of other offences taken into consideration. Rape for example, because I have the equipment in my possession, which I understand is an offence, although I have never used it.'

*   *   *

When I was a test pilot I was asked to tea by a local Judge. As I was going to the Bar, and realised that to get on well one had to know either the Law or the Judges, I accepted. It was in 1945 and when I got there the Judge asked me if I would consider standing for Parliament.

I said 'Yes, which Party have you in mind, as I know nothing about politics?'

He said 'The Liberal Party, of course.' He gave me the manifesto, which I read, and when I went to the adoption meeting I told them at the end of my speech: 'Those are my views, but they can always be changed!' I was adopted!

*   *   *

When a man is born it is said that he is kissed by an Angel on the part of his anatomy which will bring him fame and fortune. I can think of a lot of men who make excellent Chairmen, and I wonder where the Angel kissed them.

*   *   *

There are a lot of people who think HORMONES are the noises that come out of a brothel.

*   *   *

In Court a man said: the accused shouted, 'If you do that again he would break my bloody arm.' A pedantic Judge said 'I presume he said 'I will break your bloody arm' – you must correct your grammar.' 'No' said the man in the dock, 'he never mentioned your Lordship's name.'

*   *   *

The Vicar was asked to play the eunuch in a Nativity play and he refused, saying, 'Last year I had to shave off my moustache – this is going too far.'

Victor Canning
Author

Many years ago, alas, I played cricket for a village team in Kent. I prefer not to reveal the team's name. The team's captain was an eager but officious local farmer who, when we fielded, was always shouting orders to his team. One day when the opposing side was batting, the batsman hit a skyer which soared high over the slips who all converged to take the catch. Seeing this the captain shouted 'Leave it to Barnes! Leave it to Barnes'.

Obediently all the slips stood back – and then the ball fell to the ground with no one going for the catch. Our captain had forgotten that Barnes wasn't playing that week!

Dame Barbara Cartland
Author

Queen Victoria was watching the Trooping of the Colour in Horseguards' Parade with her Prime Minister, Lord Melbourne.

It was a very hot day and the heavy uniforms, especially the bearskins, and the marching up and down, made the Troops very hot.

As they passed Queen Victoria there was a very strong odour coming from the Parade. The Queen turned to Lord Melbourne and said:

'Do tell me, Lord Melbourne, what is that strong smell?'

'That, Ma'am,' he replied, 'is known as the *esprit de corps!*'

The Rt. Hon. The Lord Chalfont
P.C., O.B.E., M.C.

Politicians may be relied upon to make wise, intelligent
and statesmanlike decisions – having first exhausted all
other alternatives.

Shirley Conran
Author

Not long ago a young man arrived at Logan Airport,
Boston, hailed a cab and asked the driver where he could
'get scrod'.

The cabby thought for a minute and replied: 'You know
buddy, a lot of guys ask me that question, but you're the
first one who's ever used the pluperfect subjunctive!'

The Rt. Hon. Sir W. Allan Davis

G.B.E., F.C.A.

Lord Mayor of London, 1985–1986

I am an accountant and have long accepted that my profession presents a rather sombre image.

One day a banker and insurance broker set off in a balloon, hot air of course, for a long voyage. The winds and air currents weren't favourable and they came down rather earlier than expected. The gondola came to rest in the top of a very high tree.

A man passed underneath them and the broker called out, 'Where are we?' Quick as a flash came the reply, 'Stuck in the branches of a tree, in a balloon.' And then the man walked on.

'That man,' said the broker, 'is an accountant – you ask a perfectly sensible and simple question and his answer is absolutely accurate and useless.'

Dame Judi Dench

O.B.E.

Theatre, Film and Television Actress

It has been a wonderful dinner, and as I am no after-dinner speaker, may I offer to do the washing up.

The Rt. Hon. Lord Denning

P.C., D.L.

Master of the Rolls 1962–1982

Copy of letter received by Lord Denning from . . .
International Students' House.

Dear Lord Denning,

      I am an Indian citizen. I graduated in
Mechanical Engineering in the University of London and
was awarded a Master of Science degree. I feel I have the
necessary qualifications, motivation, energy, drive and
personality to begin a successful career in an automobile
industry. I will ever remain grateful to you if you would
kindly help me begin my professional career with your
Company, the Rolls Royce Motor Company.

Anthony Denny Esq

C.C.

Past Master of The Worshipful Company of Barbers

An Irish Mother – writing to her son

Dear Son,

Just a few lines to let you know that I'm still alive. I'm writing this letter slowly because I know you cannot read fast. You won't know the house when you come home, we've moved.

About your father, he has a lovely new job. He has 500 men under him. He is cutting the grass at the cemetery.

There was a washing machine in the new house when we moved in, but it isn't working too good. Last week I put 14 shirts into it, pulled the chain, and I haven't seen the shirts since.

Your sister, Mary, had a baby this morning. I haven't found out whether it is a boy or girl, so I don't know whether you are an aunt or an uncle.

Your Uncle Dick drowned last week in a vat of whisky in Dublin Brewery. Some of his workmates dived in to save him but he fought them off bravely. We cremated his body and it took three days for the fire to go out.

Your father didn't have much to drink at Christmas, I put a bottle of castor oil in his pint of beer. It kept him going till New Year's Day.

I went to the Doctor on Thursday and your father came with me. The Doctor put a small tube in my mouth and told me not to open it for ten minutes. Your father offered to buy it from him.

It only rained twice last week. First for three days and then for four days. Monday it was so windy that one of our chickens laid the same egg four times.

We had a letter from the undertaker. He said, if we don't pay the last instalment on your Grandmother within seven days, up she comes.

Your loving mother,

Anne Diamond
Television Presenter and Journalist

A group of Americans were in a Manhattan pub one night discussing the merits of Scotch and Irish whisky. A crowd gathered round. One man said that Scotch was much stronger than Irish. Another disagreed. 'No', he said, 'Irish whisky is dynamite. Only last week my wife and I drank a bottle of Irish whisky, got up the next morning and went to seven o'clock Mass.'

'What's unusual about that?' the other fellow asked, 'lots of people drink a bottle of whisky and get up the next day and go to Mass.'

The first guy said: 'I know, but we're Jewish.'

The Rt. Hon. Sir John Donaldson

Kt., P.C.

Master of the Rolls 1982-1992

Where a young child is to be called as a witness, the Judge has first to satisfy himself that the child knows the importance of telling the truth. On one such occasion the following dialogue took place.

Judge: 'Tommy, do you know what it is to tell the truth?'
Tommy: 'Yes.'
Judge: 'Did your mother tell you what will happen if you tell a lie?'
Tommy: 'Yes. The Judge won't find out, but God will.'

Dame Mary Donaldson

G.B.E., J.P.

Lord Mayor of London 1983–1984

I am no linguist, but I believe in making the most of my French. A friend of mine did the same when he visited the Farnborough Air Show. Finding himself next to a Frenchman, he pointed to the latest Westland product which was some way away approaching the airfield.
'Voila la Hélicoptère', he said.
'Non', replied the Frenchman – 'Le Hélicoptère'.
The Englishman looked again.
'My God, you've got good eyesight', he said.

Paul Eddington
Actor

A notice in an American university:
   No smoking in the corridors: this tradition will
   commence Monday.

The Rt. Rev. and Rt. Hon. Gerald Ellison

K.C.V.O., P.C.

Bishop of London, 1973–1981

The absent-minded professor was leaving to go to college to do his daily work, and his wife spoke to him firmly in these words:

'Now, my dear, remember that we are moving house today, and I shall be busy leaving this house and getting the new house ready to welcome you. So, don't forget, and don't come back this evening to this house. Here is our new address, and it is to this address that you are to come this evening.'

The professor duly went to college, did his work, and as was his custom, returned to his old house, forgetful of his wife's injunction. He tried to get into the house, but found all the doors locked. He peered into the windows, and saw the rooms were empty. He could not make out what had happened. Exasperated and puzzled, he wondered what to do next. He saw a boy by the gate, and called to him, telling him of his predicament, and asking if he could help.

'Oh Father', he replied, 'Mother said something like this would happen.'

The Rt. Hon. Lord Elwyn-Jones

P.C., C.H.

Lord High Chancellor of Great Britain, 1974–1979
A Lord of Appeal since 1979

On one occasion, Mr Justice Stable was about to start a criminal trial in Wales when one of those selected to be jurors put up his hand and said, 'My Lord, I am unable to serve on this jury this morning.' The Judge said, 'I am afraid I cannot release you until you explain your difficulty to me.' The juror replied, 'My wife is going to conceive this morning.' The Judge replied, 'It may be that what you are seeking to tell me is that your wife is going to be confined this morning; but whether you are right or I am right, it would seem to be an occasion at which you should personally be present.'

Sir Monty Finniston

B.Sc., Ph.D., F.R.S., F.R.S.E., F.Eng.

Industrialist

My favourite after-dinner story concerns the summit meeting at which Mr Gorbachev, President Reagan and Mrs Thatcher attended with God. Each of these national leaders was allowed to ask God one question.

Mr Gorbachev started by asking, 'When will Communism become internationally established as the sole political philosophy?' God, after a few minutes hesitation, replied: 'About the twenty-second century', and Mr Gorbachev burst into tears because he knew he would not live that long.

President Reagan then asked, 'When do you think my "star wars" researchs will come to fruition?' Again, God thought for a moment and replied, 'not until the end of the twenty-first century', at which President Reagan burst into tears because he knew he would not live that long.

Finally, Mrs Thatcher asked, 'And when do you think my monetary policy will succeed?' – and God burst into tears.

The Rt. Hon. The Earl Fortescue
J.P.

What is the first thing elephants do before they make love?

They first remove their trunks.

Christina Foyle
Owner of Foyles Bookshop

A woman asked her husband if he would marry again if she died. After some thought, he said 'yes'. 'And would you give your new wife my jewellery?' After some thought, 'yes,' 'and my fur coat' – after thought – 'Yes', 'and my golf clubs' – after thought, 'No'.

'What, you would give her my lovely jewellery, my furs – why not my golf clubs?'

'Because she is left-handed.'

*   *   *

A London cabbie having picked up a couple of American tourists at a Heathrow hotel and deposited them at the record-running thriller, 'The Mousetrap', was dismayed when he was paid the precise fare and no tip. 'The policeman did it!' he shouted after them, getting his own back.

*   *   *

An Englishman visited a brothel in Paris and on leaving, was very surprised to be handed 10,000 francs. He decided to call again the next evening and the same thing happened. On the third evening he was disappointed not to be given the francs and asked why, and was told, 'We were not televising tonight'.

*   *   *   *

Somerset Maugham talking to a girls' school about the art of writing short stories told them that the essential ingredients were religion, sex, mystery, high-rank, non-literary language and brevity.

The schoolmistress next day told her young charges to try their hand at writing one according to his recipe. After a minute one raised her hand said she had finished. The incredulous mistress told her to read it out, and she did: 'My God!', said the Duchess, 'I'm pregnant. I wonder who done it'. That girl should surely go far.

John Francome
Ex Champion National Hunt Jockey

A man goes to the doctor and tells him that he has a recurring dream where two really beautiful women keep trying to get into bed with him but he keeps pushing them both away.

The doctor enquires what the man would like him to do for his problem and the patient replies, 'Break my arms'.

W. B. Fraser

C.C.

Chairman, Royal Society of St George (City of London Branch) 1986–87

The very wealthy Chairman of a large company in Scotland visited his men on site whilst they were constructing a bridge. One well known worker passed the Chairman on the half-built structure and the Chairman noticed that the sole of his shoe was loose to the extent that it had come unstuck and was flapping as the man walked.

The Chairman called over, 'Angus – have you not got any decent walking shoes? You'll be having a serious accident with those.'

'Well, Sir,' came the reply, 'I have no money till pay day at the end of the month.'

The Chairman took a big wad of five pound notes out of his pocket, took off the elastic band and handed it to Angus saying, 'Put this around your shoe – it should make it safer.'

*   *   *

Two friends – both lorry drivers – went for interviews for a job. The first man was called in. His driving licence was inspected and the Chairman said that he only had two questions to ask.

Question one, 'What happens if you lose one eye?'

The reply was 'I could only half see'.

The second question, 'What happens if you lose the other eye?'

Reply – 'Can't see at all.'

At which point he was sent out from the interview, but as he passed his friend he said – 'Easy interview – only two questions – answer to the first one – only half see, answer to second one – can't see at all.'

His friend was called in and presented his licence etc. The Chairman then said 'You only have two questions, Question one – what happens if you lose an ear?'

Reply – 'Only half see, Sir.'

Question two – 'What happens if you lose both ears?' Prompt reply – 'Can't see at all, Sir.'

Rather amazed, the Chairman requested an explanation, to which the driver said – 'My cap would have fallen down over my eyes' – he got the job.

W. B. Fraser
C.C.

A rather grotesque elderly man was always seen escorting the most beautiful young lady.

On one occasion, he was asked, 'Where is your sex appeal?'

To which the reply was – 'In the bank.'

*   *   *

Desk sign at an office supply company:
Don't be indispensable. If you can't be replaced, you can't be promoted.

Sir David Frost

C.B.E.
Broadcaster and Author

We've just heard that at the Detroit Coliseum, Ernst Finster, the Finnish pole-vaulter, pole-vaulted a height of 19 feet 8 inches.

Unfortunately, the roof of the Detroit Coliseum was only 16 feet 5 inches high . . .

So that, in one jump, Finster broke both the indoor and outdoor records . . . as well as two collar-bones, three vertebrae and one Marley tile.

Sir Peter Gadsden

G.B.E.; M.A., D.Sc., F.Eng.
Lord Mayor of London, 1979

My period as Lord Mayor was a wonderful year, full of happy memories, many of them involving charity work and work with children.

I recall one children's Christmas party which I attended in full ceremonial garb. A little boy came up to me and asked who I was. 'I'm the Lord Mayor', I replied. 'No you're not', the little boy replied, 'there's a man over there who says he's Santa Claus, but I know he isn't really.'

Sir Ronald Gardner-Thorpe

G.B.E.

Lord Mayor of London, 1981

The Army Education Officer was in class and said 'Today we are going to discuss matters of general knowledge. You, Private Snooks, what is the difference between Slander and Libel?'

'Sir, slander is defamation of the character by the spoken word.'

'Correct, and what is libel?'

'Libel is what we Australians put on suitcases.'

*　　　*　　　*

Ascot, a very hot day, John Smith, assistant bookmaker, working extremely hard, collapsed under extreme heat and died instantly. The bookmaker himself stayed to finish the meeting and despatched his bright assistant clerk to inform Mrs. Smith. He arrived, knocked at the door: 'Are you the widow of the late John Smith?'

'No, I am not' she answered.

'Bet you 10 to 1 you are.'

*　　　*　　　*

Harry was an extremely good attender at his Livery Company, he was a member of the Court and attended all Court meetings. He started to arrive home late. It became later and later. One day he arrived back at 5.30 a.m., opened the front door, and took off his shoes. As he crept upstairs, his wife appeared from the kitchen and said 'Harry, where have you been?'

'To Court meeting my dear.'

'What, at this time!'

'Well, it was rather late, and one of the members gave me a bed.'

'Who?' No answer. When he had gone to the office she got out the little Red Book and wrote to 30 members of the Court. 'Did my Harry stay with you last night?' By return post 30 answers arrived: 'Yes, he did.'

His Honour Judge Goldstone
Recorder of the Crown Court, 1972–1978

A middle aged man had for a number of years found his secretary attractive but had never sought her social company. However, one summer his wife went on holiday on her own leaving him to his own devices on his birthday. He told his secretary of his solitude and asked her to have an early dinner with him. She agreed. They met and dined and he drove her to her flat and was invited into the hall. Looking coy the Secretary asked him if he would wait whilst she got 'everything ready'. The dinner had been pleasant, the wine good. Earlier they had started to use first names. Their hands had touched affectionately and she had looked at him in a way that made him feel twenty years younger. He was a man of the world and started to undress. Hardly had he removed the last garment when he heard through the door, 'come in Arthur'. He opened the door and walked in and saw his assembled staff as one man sang, 'Happy Birthday to you'.

The Rt. Hon. Lord Goodman

C.H., M.A.

Master of University College Oxford 1976-1986
Past Chairman of the Arts Council

Two Russian Jews managed to emigrate from Russia and arrived in New York. On arrival they found conditions not much to their taste. Everything was too intensive and rapid for them. One said to the other, 'I think we ought to go back,' to which the other replied apprehensively, 'What sort of reception would we have?', whereupon the more outgoing one suggested that he would return and send a postcard in code. The postcard would read 'I like it here; all is well'. If written in black pencil the words could be taken at their face value; if, on the other hand, he was issuing a warning that things were not all right, the postcard would be written in red pencil. To the delight of the more timid one a postcard duly arrived, written in those words with black pencil, with the additional words 'Everything is all right except that I cannot buy a red pencil.'

Alderman M. A. Graham,

Master of the Worshipful Company of Mercers 1983–1984
Sheriff of the City of London 1986–1987

A barrister was instructed to appear in an ecclesiastical court prosecuting, on behalf of the church, a vicar who insisted on calling himself Jesus Christ. The barrister travelled down to the West Country where the trial was to take place to receive instructions from the Archdeacon. In the course of the meeting the Archdeacon explained that as the Church was a bit hard up they could only afford a fee of £100 as opposed to the barrister's usual £500, but he was sure the lawyer would understand. 'Not at all', replied the lawyer, 'in a case of this importance and potential consequences the full fee was clearly justified'. 'I don't quite understand', replied the Archdeacon, 'it's a very straightforward case, you might say a foregone conclusion'. 'Ah', replied the lawyer, 'but just suppose he's right'.

Jimmy Greaves
Footballer, Author

The Arsenal football team, not enjoying a particularly good run of luck or success, was taken by their manager Don Howe on a relaxing visit to London Zoo in Regent's Park. It was to take the players' minds off a run of League defeats and a prospect in the fight to get to Wembley that was distinctly gloomy. The manager and players arrived at the crocodile pool, packed with deadly, evil, sharp-toothed creatures. After looking at them for a while it was decided to move on. All the players started to walk around the pool. The Manager, Mr Howe, took one look at the pool and calmly started to walk across it, James Bond-style. He stepped on several of the treacherous beasts and eventually made the other side, dry and none the worse for his experience which had been watched by his amazed, horrified players.

'Blimey, Boss', they chorused, 'how on earth did you do that?'

At which point Don Howe opened his jacket to display a tee-shirt upon which was written in large letters: ARSENAL FOR THE CUP!

Slowly looking at his players, he asked: 'Now lads, in all honesty you wouldn't even expect a crocodile to swallow that.'

*   *   *

Once I was sharing a television spot with a well-respected colleague. The show was live and it was a mixture of all sports: racing, ice-hockey, cricket from abroad, the lot. We were just going into a commercial break having seen a clip of a recent first division football league game, when my colleague said:

'There'll be more football later on in the programme, but after the break highlights of the Scottish Cup Final.'

Sir Desmond Heap

LL.M., Hon. LL.D.

President of the Law Society 1972–1973

The Guest of Honour (replying for the Guests) had gone
on (mostly about himself) for some thirty-five minutes.
The Master (in the Chair) then rose to close the evening's
proceedings. Said the Master, 'I'm sure I speak for all
when I say how greatly we enjoyed Sir Billhook's moving
and comprehensive address. We really must remember to
ask him again – when he has less time.'

Rachael Heyhoe Flint

M.B.E.

Journalist, Broadcaster, Public Speaker, Sportswoman

A farmer's wife was epecting a baby and the town doctor was called out in the dead of night to the remote farmhouse, miles from anywhere, and without such modern attributes as electricity.

The doctor delivered the baby, and the nervous farmer was called to assist. He stood holding the oil lamp in order to give the doctor light. 'Hold the lamp closer', said the doctor – and within minutes a boy was born. 'Hang on a minute,' said the doctor, 'I think you are going to have twins – bring the lamp closer.' And soon a twin baby girl came into the world. The farmer was still recovering from the shock when the doctor cried, 'Hold on a minute, I do believe you are going to have triplets; come closer with the lamp.' Lo and behold, another baby boy appeared to complete the triplets. The farmer sat slumped in a chair. 'Good heavens,' said the doctor, 'I think it could be quads . . . come closer and hold the lamp.' 'Not blooming likely,' said the farmer, 'I'm not that stupid; it's the blasted light which keeps attracting them.'

Michael Hill

Q.C.

Chairman of the Criminal Bar Association 1982-1986
Chairman of the Investment Committee 1991-2001

There was this American judge who had to try a very important civil action that was bound to attract a great deal of public attention and was going to do the loser a great deal of harm. It involved allegations of corruption in high places. About a week before the trial, the defendant sneaked into the judge's Chambers and pressed $15,000 into his hand, gave him a knowing look and left without saying a word. The judge put the money into his pocket. The day before the trial, the plaintiff learnt what had happened, himself crept into the Chambers, pressed $20,000 into the judge's hand and left without saying a word. The following day, in Court, the judge handed back to the plaintiff $5,000. When asked to explain why, he said that it was important that there should be no suggestion that he was biased in favour of one party or the other!

*   *   *

Very grand English High Court judge on Assize was entertained one balmy night by the High Sheriff, who, in the judge's view, was very much one of the nouveau riche and a most awful bore.

They ate in a beautiful dining room, with French doors opening onto landscaped garden, vast and immaculately-kept lawn sweeping down to a pretty, tinkling stream. It was a superb meal, with great wine but appalling conversation. Half way through the meal migrating geese flew overhead. The High Sheriff listened intently to them and then said, very sadly, 'I don't understand it. They never stop here. I put food out for them and everything and they still never stop.' The High Court judge, just under his breath, muttered, 'Bloody snobs!'

Admiral of the Fleet The Lord Hill-Norton
G.C.B., K.C.B., C.B.

A rather pompous and unpopular Minister was in the habit of reading his speeches directly from the text produced by his officials, and seldom took the trouble to read them through – much less check or amend them – before delivery.

There came the day in the House when he had to open an awkward debate on a complicated industrial re-organisation. Text in hand, pages and pages of it, he ploughed doggedly on, enjoying the well-turned phrases setting out the manifold difficulties facing his Department in resolving this highly contentious problem, until at the bottom of page 13 he reached the magic words '. . . and now Mr Speaker, having set out the problem I come to my proposed solution'. Turning to page 14 he found, in manuscript in the middle of the page, 'Now you are on your own you bastard'.

*   *   *

The monthly political indoctrination meeting at a steel-works in a small town in one of the land-locked Iron Curtain countries had pursued its usual turgid course for most of its allotted four hours, when the Party Official finally asked for questions from the floor. A voice at the back piped up,

'Why do we not have a Minister for the Navy?'

'What a foolish question comrade', replied the Commissar, 'surely you know that we haven't got a Navy'.

'But that is no answer mate', came back the cry,

'We have a Minister of Justice'.

The Rt. Hon. Baron Home of The Hirsel
P.C.
Prime Minister, 1963

There was a bishop who declined the invitation to say Grace as he didn't want God to know that he was present.

Antony Hopkins

C.B.E.

Composer, Conductor and Broadcaster

In one of the small universities that mushroomed up in the 'sixties and are relentlessly being closed down in the 'eighties, there was a small music department with a professor, a couple of assistants and a dozen or so students reading for their music degree. To acquire such a degree one is expected to write a substantial work, a symphony, concerto or choral piece with orchestra. One student went to his professor in despair. 'I can do the history and the theory and the counterpoint but I can't write a major work – I'm not a composer at all . . .' 'My dear boy', said the professor, 'I've heard that story many a time and I have the perfect solution. What you do is this; buy the score of a fairly obscure, slightly modern (but not too much so) symphony, and simply copy it out backwards; believe me, it'll look quite convincing and they don't have time to look at it all that closely. Get it nicely bound – they do appreciate that, and if you can afford it a little gilt around the edges helps. Presentation is just as important as content . . .'

The student was deeply grateful, and as a token of his devotion bought his professor's one published symphony. He spent his whole summer vacation copying it out backwards, only to discover to his dismay that he had a handwritten copy of Sibelius's Fourth.

Sir Edward Howard

B.T., G.B.E.

Lord Mayor of London, 1971

Some years ago, the late Lord Derby presided at the
Annual General Meeting of a charity at the Mansion
House. He was a delightful man and a good Chairman
but he was very heavily built, weighing around twenty
stone. At the conclusion of the meeting, the then Bishop
of London, the Reverend Montgomery-Campbell rose
and said, 'Ladies and Gentlemen I have been asked to
propose a vote of thanks to Lord Derby for taking the
Chair. However, I really think I ought to propose a vote
of thanks to the chair for taking Lord Derby.'

Sir David Hunt

K.C.M.G., O.B.E.

In 1942 Churchill was entertaining at lunch William
Temple, recently appointed Archbishop of Canterbury.
At about that time the Germans had carried out some
raids on places such as Bath which were known as 'the
Baedeker raids' because it was thought they were
directed against cities which were peculiarly part of the
British cultural inheritance. Churchill's mind turned to
the subject of raids on Canterbury and he asked the
Archbishop what he did. 'What you ought to do', he
went on without pausing for an answer, 'is to take shelter
in the crypt of the Cathedral. I know it well. There you
would be protected not only by the massive vault of the
crypt but also by the whole structure of the Cathedral
above, and you should be safe from anything except a
direct hit from an armour-piercing bomb. And if, my dear
Archbishop, while you were sheltering in the crypt it did
receive a direct hit from an armour-piercing bomb, then
that you should regard as in the nature of a summons'.

The Rt. Hon. Douglas Hurd

C.B.E., P.C., M.P.
Writer and Retired Politician

An old American lady was travelling in a Aeroflot airliner from Moscow to London. The steward came into the cabin while the plane was over Poland and said: 'Unfortunately one of our engines has collapsed and we will be half an hour late in London as a result'.

The plane flew on.

Over East Germany the same steward appeared and said: 'Unfortunately the second engine is no longer functioning and therefore we shall be one hour late in reaching London.'

The plane flew on.

When the plane was over West Germany the same steward appeared and said: 'Unfortunately the pilot has asked me to tell you that the third engine is now no longer working with the result that we shall be two hours late arriving in London.'

The old lady said: 'Gee, I hope nothing happens to the fourth engine, or we shall be up here all night'.

Rufus Ide

C.C.

Master of the Worshipful Company of Glass Sellers, 1964

Doctor to Patient: 'I am very sorry to say that I have rather a bad piece of news for you, in fact I have two'
Patient: 'Oh dear, what is it?'
Doctor: 'You have only twenty-four hours to live.'
Patient: 'Good Heavens, what other piece of bad news could there be?'
Doctor: 'I was trying to get you on the telephone all day yesterday.'

*   *   *

Patient: 'It's my piles Doctor . . .'
Doctor: 'Yes, well let me see. Yes, Hum, Yes, Indeed.'
Doctor goes to a corner of the room and takes a long pole with a heavy brass hook on the end.
Patient leaps from his chair and asks: 'What are you going to do Doctor?'
Doctor: 'I am only just going to open the window.'

*   *   *

The King was in the garden digging up the spuds,
The Queen was in the laundry washing out his duds,
The Maid was in the parlour eating bread and honey,
When along comes Clive Jenkins and gets her more money.

*   *   *

Hitler's ghost returns to earth and is astonished to find the Jews fighting and the Germans making money.

*   *   *

An Economist is a man who knows 364 ways of making love but has no woman.

*   *   *

If you laid all the Economists round the world end to end you would not have reached a conclusion.

*   *   *

An Ornithological Meteorologist is a man who looks at birds and can tell weather.

*   *   *

Venus is receiving guests at a party in her apartment on Mount Olympus. A magnificent naked man rides up bareback on a huge white horse, but this does not cause the stir he had hoped, and in a great voice he shouts, 'I am Thor.'

Venus, 'I am not Thurprised you thilly boy, try widing thide thaddle next time.'

Jayne Irving
TV Newsreader

Two extremely well-known Shakespearean actors were taking part in a double-headed afternoon and evening performance of one of the Bard's great tragi-histories. Both men were fond of a drink, so fond indeed that the play's director and producer had been forced to devise a scheme to prevent the two from leaving the theatre between the afternoon session and the evening one, fearing the consequences. Alas! One day our heroes escaped and made their way to a local pub, where they drank liberally of the available wines, ales and spirits.

Back at the theatre they prepared for the evening play. It fell to one of them to appear on stage, alone, with the curtain as a backdrop, to speak the Prologue: a well-known device to bring the audience up to date with developments they might not have been aware of. Enter Hero Number One to begin the said Prologue . . .

Well, it became clear after a few lines that he was not going to make it. He tried several times. He thought of paraphrasing the iambics, but to no avail. He swayed, he staggered, he damn near fell over. In the embarrassed silence that greeted his efforts, an angry voice from the stalls was heard to say: 'Dammit, you're drunk, sir.'

To which our hero, mindful of his mid-afternoon drinking companion, drew himself up to a dignified Shakespearean mien and declared: 'You think I'm drunk. Wait 'til you see the bloody Duke of Gloucester.'

The Very Reverend Lawrence Jackson
Provost Emeritus of Blackburn

The trains from Tunbridge Wells, which leave seemingly
every other minute in the early morning, carry
prestigious commuters to Cannon Street and Charing
Cross. The majority of the carriages are first-class and it is
known that the occupants travel on the same train, sitting
in the same seats and reading the same newspapers,
sometimes for twenty-five or thirty years! The significant
thing about the Tunbridge Wells commuters is that they
remain totally silent and apparently inarticulate and, it is
said, will travel with the same companions for
twenty-five or thirty years without saying a word!

On a certain morning, one of the commuters,
bowler-hatted and briefcased, with a tightly rolled
umbrella, had no sooner taken his usual seat than he
announced to his three travelling companions that on the
following day he was to retire. Having said nothing at all
across many years, he judged this was the right time for
him to become articulate and to describe to his travelling
companions details of his name, his occupation and his
circumstances.

In military fashion, he commanded his immediate
neighbour to lower his copy of the *Financial Times*. Then
to his companion's shocked amazement he declared, 'I
want you to know that I am a Brigadier, I am married, I
have four sons, and they are all doctors – what about
that?'

With the *Financial Times* quivering on his lap, the
traveller thus addressed blurted out, 'How
extraordinary, I also am a Brigadier; I am married;
likewise I have four sons, and they are all dental
surgeons!'

The two newly-vocal travellers now rounded on the
third occupant in his traditional seat. He had already
lowered his copy of the *Daily Telegraph* and addressed the
other occupants of the carriage with the words, 'I also am

a Brigadier; I also am married; more remarkably, I likewise have four sons and they are all in insurance!'

There was only one remaining occupant of the carriage, whose head was buried in the *Daily Mirror*. Without removing the newspaper, he addressed his three companions with the words: 'All right then, I am a Sergeant Major; I am *NOT* married; I have four sons – and they are all BRIGADIERS!'

David Jacobs
D.L.
Radio Broadcaster

Quite recently, sitting in my club (which for the sake of the story shall be nameless), I overhead two Bishops at tea. One said to the other: 'There is no doubt in my mind whatsoever that I do not approve of sex before marriage.' The other Bishop put down his tea-cup and said quite solemnly, 'I totally agree with you, I didn't sleep with my wife before we were married. Did you?' The other Bishop looked him straight in the eyes and said, 'I really can't remember – what was her name?'

P. D. James

O.B.E.

Author

A Frenchman, an Englishman and an American were in deep trouble in some remote country and were all sentenced to be guillotined. The Frenchman was asked if he would like to face upwards to the blade, or down to the earth. He said that he would prefer to gaze at the good soil of France. The knife descended, but an inch from his neck it quivered and stuck. The officer in charge congratulated him and said that under the law of the country he was entitled to be reprieved.

The next candidate for execution was the Englishman. He said that he wasn't afraid to see what was coming to him and would look upward to the blade, but again it stuck just above his throat and he too was reprieved.

Lastly came the American. He said that he was just as prepared as any Limey to face what was coming to him, and that he would look upward. Just as the executioner was about to release the blade he put up his finger and said: 'Hi! Hold on a minute. I think I can see what the trouble is here.'

(The advantage of this story is that it can be adapted to suit different audiences, different nationalities and different professions.)

Alderman Brian Jenkins

M.A., F.C.A.

The Great Survivor
Talleyrand was probably the greatest survivor of all. A Bishop in ancient regime France; survived the revolution; Napoleon's foreign minister; principal French negotiator afterward at the Congress of Vienna. Still alive during the next revolution in 1830.

'Who are winning?' he was asked.

'We are.'

'Who are we, my Lord?'

'Ask me tomorrow and I will tell you.'

Sir Anthony Jolliffe

G.B.E.

Lord Mayor of London, 1982

Fish and Chip Story

It was not long ago that we were at a function which finished at 11 o'clock – it was not in the City and we did not get anything to eat. We arrived back at the Mansion House, the Lady Mayoress, myself and Colonel Brooke Johnson at 11.15 p.m. and I said 'I'm hungry' and the Colonel said 'It's all right Lord Mayor, we will wait until the morning.' I said 'I'm not waiting till the morning. I want something to eat' and he said 'You won't get anything to eat at this time of night because they lock everything up at the Mansion House at about 8.00 p.m. when there is nothing on here. Although you get accommodation you don't get food with it. It is not bed and breakfast. It's just bed.'

I said 'Well I have the answer, I have an account with a taxi company in London.'

So I rang them up and I said 'Can you please deliver three dover sole and chips?' and the fellow said 'What's your name?' I said "Jolliffe." 'Where do you want them delivered?'

Well that was a problem. I said 'The Mansion House, side door.' He said 'The what?' I said 'The Mansion House.' He said 'Where is that?' I said 'It's in the City'. 'Oh' he said, 'we will ring you back.'

Well that was another problem because I didn't want them to know downstairs what I was doing. So I rang down to the telephonist here and I said to him 'I have got a parcel being delivered in about half an hour by taxi.' I said 'when they deliver it, let me know and I will come down and fetch it. I don't want to disturb anybody at this time of night.'

Well, about fifteen minutes later the telephone went and the chap on the switchboard here said: 'Lord Mayor, they cannot find any dover sole and chips.' I said 'Are they still on the line?' He said no. I said 'Get them back.'

They came back on and I said 'Look, I know where there is a fish and chip shop just down off the Haymarket.' He said: 'Look here mate.' He said 'some geezer is messing us about. We just had a call that the Lord Mayor of London wants three dover sole and chips. We are not being mucked about at this time of night.'

I said, 'Well actually, the Lord Mayor of London *does* want three dover sole and chips.' He said, 'Who are you?' I said, 'I'm the Lord Mayor of London.' He said, 'Blimey, it's not my night. I said 'It's not ours either.'

So there you are – a night in the life of the Lord Mayor of London.

John Junkin
Actor and Broadcaster

A young man is being shown around a computer firm and is introduced to the most up-to-date and sophisticated computer in the world. He is told that he may ask it any question, on any subject, and it is guaranteed to come up with the correct answer.

The young man asks the computer, 'Where is my father?' and within a second the computer replies, 'Playing golf at Sunningdale'.

'Incorrect,' says the young man, 'My father is dead'.

'The man your mother married is dead,' says the computer, 'Your father is playing golf at Sunningdale.'

Henry Kelly
Broadcaster

Generally, I prefer turns of phrase rather than 'jokes'. My mother had a great one: if ever we complained at home she'd say: 'This family doesn't know how well off it is . . . it's down on your knees you should all be, thanking God you're on your feet.' The Irish don't mean to be funny when they speak. They just talk that way. They ask you questions like: 'Where were you going yesterday when I saw you on your way to work?'

And without waiting for a reply they said: 'I wanted to talk to you, but when I caught up with you, you were gone.' Or you meet a Hall Porter in a posh hotel who picks up your bags to assist you to your room. Minding his manners he says: 'Follow me, sir, I'll be right behind you.'

If I do have a story it comes from a distinguished Irish writer and dramatist Hugh Leaonard, author of many hit plays which have been brought to the stage of London and New York and onto the world's television screens. He once told me he was staying in a hotel in Cork and was in the shower early one morning when there was a knock on the door.

'Who is it?' he asked.

'It's Danny, the porter' came the reply, 'I have an urgent telegram for you.'

'I'm in the shower, Danny,' said Hugh, 'would you just slip it in under the door please.'

'I can't do that Mr Leaonard,' said Danny, 'it's on a tray.'

Ludovic Kennedy
Writer and Broadcaster

At a trial, Counsel asked a witness who was a sailor whether a certain event had surprised him. 'Surprised?' he replied, 'Why, you could have b......d me through me oilskins.'

The Judge leaned over to Counsel and said, 'I think he means he was taken aback.'

His Honour Alan King-Hamilton
Judge, Q.C.

A barrister had been addressing the Court of Appeal for two and a half days on a very dull point of law. At the end of his argument, which he feared had not been acceptable to the Court, he expressed the hope that their Lordships would not think he had been wasting the time of the Court – 'Wasting the Court's time?' said the presiding Lord Justice, 'You have trespassed upon eternity!'

The Rev. Dr. B. A. C. Kirk-Duncan

Rector of St. Mary-at-Hill City of London, Former President of Sion College

Two senior retired Army Officers were chatting in their Club about the shortcomings of the modern generation.

'Do you know', said the General, 'I was telling my daughter-in-law that my grandfather was killed at Waterloo. She looked up with a sympathetic expression and said:

'Oh, how sad. On what platform did it happen?'

'Ridiculous', said the Brigadier, 'as if it mattered what platform he was on.'

The Hon. Sir John Latey

M.B.E.

Past Judge of The High Court of Justice

Until towards the end of last century the High Court
Judges of the Chancery Division used to go out on
Assize, as well as those of the other Divisions, to try all
the mixed bags of cases that came along, including
criminal ones. But both as barristers practising at the
Chancery Bar and on promotion to the Bench their work
was of a highly specialist, not to say esoteric, nature.
They were not worldly men in those days.

They ceased going on Assizes because, it is said,
probably apocryphally, of a rape prosecution tried by a
Chancery Judge with a jury.

At the beginning of the hearing, Prosecuting Counsel
suggested that the case be heard *in camera* as the facts
were sordid. The Judge asked Defending Counsel
whether he agreed, and he did. He asked the jury, and
they agreed. Then he asked the accused. Try as he would
he could not get the accused to understand what *in camera*
meant. 'Very well' said the Judge, 'Prosecuting Counsel
understands what I mean, your Counsel understands
what I mean, the jury understand what I mean. The
hearing will proceed in camera'.

It did, and the time came for the accused to give his
evidence. He related how he met the girl, suggested a
walk, she agreed, they went down a lane into a field and
got down behind a haystack.

'And' said the accused, 'I gave it her hot and strong'.
'You did what?' said the Judge, 'I do not understand you'.
'Well, sir, I let her have it good and hearty'.
'You let her have what?' said the Judge. 'I do not
understand you. Can't you speak the Queen's English?'
'Well, sir' said the accused, 'Prosecuting Counsel
understands what I mean. Defending Counsel understands
what I mean. The Jury understand what I mean. And if you'd
been there with your bloody camera so would you.'

A 'Lawyer Friend'

It is not true that villains are necessarily irreligious. Many subscribe to the Commandment:

'Do unto others as you would they should do unto you.'

It is true, however, that a number of them add the words:

'. . . but do them first.'

Another 'Lawyer Friend'

A schoolmaster correcting examination papers received from one candidate 10 foolscap sheets of paper which were blank except for the words on each one: 'Macbeth Act 2 Scene 5 Line 28'. He could hardly contain his curiosity, but eventually went to the Senior Common Room, found his collected works of Shakespeare, looked up the reference to Macbeth and found that the line read:
  'I cannot do this bloody thing.'

*　　　*　　　*

A friend, whose word of regard was totally unreliable, told me that he was going up in a lift in one of our big stores when, at the fourth floor, a young lady entered, wearing nothing except a pair of shoes and carrying a handbag. He managed to contain his embarrassment until they reached the sixth floor when, with great tact, he turned to the lady and said, 'Madam, may I be permitted to say how much I admire your outfit. My wife has got one at home that is just the same, but somehow it doesn't seem to fit quite so well.'

*　　　*　　　*

Physicians are men who know everything but do nothing.
Surgeons are men who know nothing but do everything.
Pathologists are men who know everything and do everything but 24 hours too late.

*　　　*　　　*

LITTLE SNIPPETS
Speaking generally, lawyers are generally speaking.

*　　　*　　　*

It is strange that the period when traffic is almost at a standstill is called 'the rush hour'.

*   *   *

The big problem with airlines is seats – getting ours into theirs.

*   *   *

Life is full of disappointments: nothing ever seems to come off – except buttons.

*   *   *

A gentleman is a person who has learned to play his accordion – but doesn't.

*   *   *

Notice outside hospital – 'Beware – Guard Dogs operating'.

*   *   *

Definition of a person who lacks modesty:
A person who answers his own prayers.
A person who sends a telegram of congratulations to his mother on his birthday.

*   *   *

There was an Irish gambler who lost £600 on the St. Leger, £200 on the race and £400 on the action replay.

*   *   *

After Dr Coggan had retired, one of his God-children is reputed to have said: 'I haven't got an Archbishop as a Godfather any longer, he's retarded.'
    (Dr. Coggan tells me he does not recall the former, but vouches for the latter!)

Sir Christopher Leaver

G.B.E.

Lord Mayor of London 1981

During the time of the recession a businessman took a taxi the 78 miles from his home in Dover to London. When he reached his destination he apologised to the driver for being unable to pay the fare but added that, as he was appearing at a meeting of his creditors, the taxi driver was welcome to attend.

*   *   *

I am a wine merchant. At the time of the recession even my customers who didn't intend to pay stopped ordering.

*   *   *

When I lived in the Mansion House I regularly dressed for dinner in tail coat, breeches, stockings, silver-buckled shoes, jabot and decorations; standard uniform for a Lord Mayor. One evening as I was leaving for a function, my five-year-old daughter said, 'Oh, Daddy, you're not wearing those clothes again, you know they always give you a headache in the morning.'

The Rt. Hon. Lord Mancroft

K.B.E., T.D., M.A.

Barrister and Author

Some weeks ago I was rung up by the Secretary of a Students Law Debating Society of which I had been a member in my youth.

'Lord Mancroft', he said, 'will you please give us your advice. Do you know the Lord Chancellor?' 'Yes, of course', I replied. 'Why do you ask?' 'Well', he said, 'tell us quite frankly. Do you think he will be offended if we ring him up at a moment's notice and ask him to take the place at our annual dinner of our guest of honour who has fallen sick.'

'That,' I said, 'depends greatly on the calibre of the guest who's fallen sick. I mean, if you've succeeded in attracting to your dinner somebody outside the normal run of after-dinner speakers – someone like Fidel Castro or Marlene Dietrich – well then, I suppose he might in a light-hearted way, consider it. Who is your stricken guest of the evening?' They mentioned the name of a Mr Bert Briggins, or somebody I had never heard of in my life before.

'Good Heavens', I said, 'you can't do that to a man of Lord Hailsham's standing. He'll be mortally offended. Outraged'.

'Oh, Lord Mancroft', said the Secretary, 'thank you so much for speaking so frankly. You have stopped us from making fools of ourselves and prevented us from dropping a dreadful brick. Lord Mancroft, we suppose you wouldn't like to come and make the speech for us?'

The Rt. Hon. The Lord Marsh

P.C., F.C.I.T.

Chairman, British Railways Board, 1971–1976

A tired and emotional politician was the guest of a President of a South American country. The dinner was even more boring than usual. At its conclusion, the guests mingled and, to his delight, the orchestra burst into a lively melody. His face lit up and he turned to a vision in a beautiful flowing red robe, put his arms out and said, 'Come on, let's dance.' His intended partner pushed him away and brusquely refused the invitation.

When the politician asked why his intended partner was so unfriendly he received the reply, 'For three reasons; one – you are drunk; two – we are listening to my country's National Anthem, and, three – I am the Papal Nuncio!'

Alderman Clive Martin
Publisher

FROM THE SEA

One of the problems of crossing the ocean, whether on a holiday cruise or on a troopship, is providing suitable entertainment for the passengers. One shipping line employed a very clever magician whose fame was legendary. At least, it was until one day he found himself on a ship, the captain of which, in the older seafaring tradition, had a parrot.

This parrot had the run of the ship, although he had been advised by the captain to keep clear of the galley! One of the parrot's favourite occupations was to sit at the back of the entertainment hall during the magician's shows. Unfortunately, the parrot, having seen it all many times, had a very irritating habit of calling out the whereabouts of the disappearing rabbit, playing card, coloured handkerchief or ball, just at the moment the audience was spellbound and about to burst into applause. There was nothing the magician could do. He had thought many times of strangling the bird, but decided such a step might not be popular with the captain!

One day, however, during one of these shows, the ship unhappily struck a rock and sank, leaving everybody in the water, including the parrot. After swimming about in search of his master, a very bedraggled parrot clambered on to one of the rafts and, much to his surprise, found himself face to face with the magician. He stared at the magician for a very long time, until suddenly the parrot broke the silence by saying: 'All right, Mr Clever magician, I give up! What have you done with the boat?'

Christopher Martin-Jenkins
BBC Radio and Television Cricket Commentator,
Cricket correspondent for *The Times*

An American, Walter J. Kreitzberger, was walking down a street in New York last week when he came across a shoe shop and remembered that he had left a pair of shoes there to be repaired on the day he was conscripted into the U.S. Army in 1943. Just out of interest he went into the shop and asked if they still had any shoes belonging to a Mr Kreitzberger that had been left for repair.

'What was the name again?' asked the man in an apron behind the counter.

'Kreitzberger.'

The shopkeeper frowned and mumbled under his breath as he flicked through the pages of a big dusty book. 'Kreitzberger, Kreitzberger . . . How are you spelling that?'

'K-R-E-I-T-Z-B-E-R-G-E-R', replied the American.

'Is that Walter J. Kreitzberger of Lexicon Avenue, Manhattan?'

'That's me!' said Walter, astonished.

The shopkeeper smiled up at the American and said, 'Okay, fella, they'll be ready on Tuesday.'

Julia McKenzie
Actress and Singer

In the wilds of Ireland, a young couple asked the way from an old local. 'Well', he said, 'it's first on the right, then go along till you can see Sean O'Grady's pig, then it's five miles up the next road on the left, take the right fork, then . . . no, it'll be quicker if you go through the town, take the next right after the pub, go along five hundred yards till you reach . . . do you have to start from here?'

Norris D. McWhirter

C.B.E.
Author, Publisher and Broadcaster

THE BOTTOM LINE

A senior civil servant and his wife celebrate his retirement and their ruby wedding. They return on a sentimental journey to the Yorkshire dale where they spent their honeymoon just after the war. Tragically, Lady Carruthers has 'a turn' and expires.

Sir Humphrey decides that she should be buried in the little churchyard overlooking the route of their last walk together. For the headstone he selects their favourite stanza by Andrew Marvel (1621–1678)

> All this, and soft and sweet
> Which scattering doth shine
> Shall within one beauty meet
> And she was thine'

The arrangements for the 'family only' burial are completed with the vicar. The family are horrified by a misprint on the headstone which reads:

> 'And she was thin'

Rather than worry the vicar, Sir Humphrey seeks out the mason in his cottage to request him just to add the missing 'e'. The next summer he journeys north to pay the verger's wife for tending the grave. He is checking to see everything is in order. He pushes down the grass to check that the bottom line has been attended to. With disbelief he reads:

> 'And E she was thin'

Alderman Francis McWilliams
Past Master of The Worshipful Company of Arbitrators

Angus and Kirstie lived in a remote village in the
Highlands. Every evening Angus came to call and the
pair went for a walk up the glen. This had been the
pattern for 14 years and there had been no discussion of
matrimony.

On this particular evening the moon was full and the
air was warm and soft. Truly a night made for lovers.
And, as they say in those parts, 'Kirstie fell from grace'.
Afterwards, as they returned down the glen, not a word
was exchanged between them. When they reached the
gate of her cottage Kirstie could contain herself no longer.
'Angus' she said in a voice filled with emotion, 'Ye'll be
thinking that I'm nothing but a common prostitute'.
Clearly alarmed, Angus replied, 'Now, now Kirstie, there
was no talk of remuneration'.

Cliff Michelmore

C.B.E., F.R.S.A.

Television Broadcaster and Producer

Each one of us could tell what delights us. Coming home to roast beef and Yorkshire pudding after a month in deepest fried America is one of my delights. To an American it might be getting back to the 'ball game'. To a Frenchman, having a wife and a mistress BOTH of whom 'understand' him.

To a Russian it is being woken up at four o'clock in the morning, having the bedroom door knocked down by four KGB men, one of whom stands at the foot of the bed and says, 'Ivan Ivanovitch, you are under arrest, come with us.'

The delight is to be able to reply: 'Ivan Ivanovitch lives next door.'

*   *   *

Advice to any new after-dinner speaker. If you have not struck oil after five minutes, stop boring and sit down.

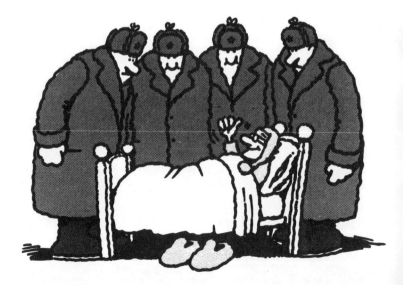

George Mikes LL.D.
Author

The first criterion of a good after dinner speech is that, obviously, it must be a good story. But it increases its snob-value if you can add casually: 'I've heard that from Prince Philip . . .' or someone else really worth mentioning. I once heard Lord Birkett, the judge – perhaps the finest after-dinner speaker of a bygone decade – boasting that he had heard a particular story from Tommy Trinder (for the sake of younger readers: a successful comedian on a not too high intellectual level). Judges, Princes, Professors, Birkett knew galore, but of Trinder's acquaintance he was inordinately proud.

*   *   *

I have heard this story from Lord Carrington. Where did I meet Lord Carrington? I met him – a further excellent point for a speech – at the 300th Annual Dinner of the Royal Society. Why was I invited at all? A good question: for 299 years they had ignored me. The simple explanation is that one of the guests of honour, who replied to a toast, was the President of the Hungarian Academy of Science and they decided to invite a few more Hungarians lest the illustrious guest should feel too lonely.

So here is the story which I heard from Lord Carrington at the annual dinner of the Royal Society.

When Carrington was appointed Secretary General of NATO he had to visit a number of high ranking officers, among them a general in his Sussex home. They were having a drink (or two) when a ravishingly beautiful blonde-haired woman came in.

'Meet my wife', said the general. Carrington stood up, was only too pleased to meet the lady who left the two men after a few minutes. Soon afterwards another – I cannot say even more, but just as ravishingly beautiful, blonde-haired lady joined them, obviously the twin sister of the general's wife. The general said, 'Meet my sister-in-law'. Carrington was speechless. When he regained his voice, he asked, 'But how on earth can you tell them apart?' To which the general replied, gruffly, 'That's their problem, not mine.'

Sir John Mills

C.B.E.

Actor, Author, Producer, Director

I've always been keenly conscious of how lucky I am
(touch wood: like most actors I am ridiculously
superstitious – never walk under ladders, never whistle
in the dressing-room, always throw salt over my left
shoulder if any spills on the table, etc.) to have been
working for the past 50 years in a profession that is still so
enthralling and stimulating that retirement is
unthinkable. Like the old soldier, I should simply fade
away.

Sir John Gielgud, not long ago, was questioned by a
reporter on the subject of retirement. 'Sir John, you are
over seventy, still playing long parts and acting them
with your usual brilliance. If, God forbid, at some time in
the hopefully long-distant future your memory begins to
fail and you find it impossible to remember your lines, I
suppose you will be forced reluctantly to retire'.

Sir John regarded the reporter with a slightly
incredulous look on his face and replied: 'My dear fellow,
there's always the radio!'

John Minchall-Fogg

Journalist, Hon. Secretary and Vice Chairman of the
Royal Society of St. George (City of London Branch)

This is a story about the nouveau-riche golfer and the
Scottish caddie. His man was a bad golfer by any
standards, but would not give up. Standing on the first
tee at a famous course, the parvenu hit the first ball into
the facing lake. Undaunted, he opened his golf bag, took
out another new ball and hit that one too, straight into
deep water. He did so again and again and again, until
even the caddie's heart softened to the beginner. 'Will ye
no try with an old ball?' he asked. It was with sorrow, not
anger, that his master replied plaintively: 'When you play
like I do you don't *have* any *old* balls.'

*   *   *

A vicar, whose flock included two cricket clubs, was
playing rather well for one of them and on the way to
winning the match, when a ball, pitched well outside the
wicket, struck him via his bat on his front pad. ''Ow's
that?' asked the bowler. 'Out, l.b.w.' said the umpire,
past whom the vicar wended his sorrowing way to the
pavilion. It was, naturally enough, the fielding club's
umpire but, worse than that, he was the vicar's own
sextant. 'George, George', said the departing cleric, 'I fear
you'll never get to Heaven.' 'Don't you worry vicar',
replied George, 'I never 'ad no 'ead for 'eights.'

Sir Patrick Moore

O.B.E.

Radio and Television Broadcaster and Author

A beautiful princess lived in a castle with the King and the Queen. One day she went down to the pool, and found a frog which was clearly very ill. She tried to nurse it back to health, but it was slow to recover, and eventually she took it back into the castle. When she went to bed, she took the frog with her to keep it warm. In the morning the frog had turned into a handsome prince. The prince and the princess married and lived happily every after.

But the King and the Queen never did believe the story about the frog!

Stirling Moss

O.B.E., F.I.E.

Racing Motorist 1947-1962

A man is abandoned on a desert island. After he's been there for five years, a beautiful blonde in a wet suit is washed ashore. He goes with interest to appraise the new arrival. After she has composed herself, they get into conversation. 'How long have you been here?' she asks. 'Five years.' he replies. 'A long time then,' she says, 'would you like a drink?' 'I'd love one,' he answers and, with that, she unzips a pocket in her wet suit and produces a bottle of scotch. 'When you were back in the big world, did you smoke?' asks the blonde. 'Yes.' he says. 'Would you like a cigarette then?' And with that, she unzips another pocket and produces cigarettes and a lighter. Our desert island dweller is now in seventh heaven, lying back on the sand, enjoying a double scotch and a good smoke. The lady then asks 'How long did you say you've been here?' 'Five years.' comes the reply. 'Ah,' she says, 'then . . . would you like to play around?' His response to this suggestion . . . 'Don't tell me you've got the golf clubs in there as well!'

Cyril Murkin
O.B.E.
Deputy

A specialist found amongst those waiting in his surgery a lady of gigantic proportions, really hanging with fat! He found to his horror that he was called upon to explore her rear end. Aftr shuffling for some while, he finally addressed the lady: 'Madam, it would assist me greatly if you could lift your buttock up.' 'Ah,' quoth the lady, 'Doctor, I'm afraid I have no idea where my buttercup is!'

*　　　*　　　*

A nouveau riche lady was called to the hospital where her husband, she was informed, had to be given artificial respiration!

'Doctor,' she said, 'we are not paupers – give him the real thing, we can afford it.'

The Rt. Hon. Sir Patrick Nairne
G.C.B., K.C.B., M.C., M.A., P.C.
Master, St. Catharine's College Oxford and Hon. LL.D.

I once accompanied a politician with whom I worked in Whitehall to a public meeting at which he had to make an important address. The acoustics were not very good and, after he had been speaking for about five minutes, he paused and asked: 'Can you hear me at the back?' The politician was somewhat nonplussed when a man at the back of the room shouted as a reply: 'I can hear you alright, but I am quite ready to change places with somebody who can't.'

Sir David Napley
Past President of The Law Society

A woman entered the open door of a suburban house and saw a little boy on the floor playing with his train.

'You won't know me', she said, 'but I'm your grandmother on your father's side'. 'Well', said the little boy without looking up,

'I can tell you this now. You're on the wrong side'.

*   *   *

You can always rely on the newspapers for complete accuracy in reporting. Having described a romance which had blossomed between an actor and an actress appearing locally in a pre-run London production, a Cheshire paper concluded 'The leading lady and her leading man will be married next Saturday afternoon. The usual performance will take place in the evening'.

J. E. Neary

F.R.I.C.S.

President of the City Livery Club 1984,
Sheriff of the City of London 1985–1986
Past Master of The Worshipful Company of Shipwrights

My favourite after-dinner story is the tale concerning Henry Ford in the Mid-West in the mid-thirties.

Travelling on business he arrived in a small, in the geographical sense, but big in every other sense, town where the local convent had a fund-raising campaign to build a small old-people's home alongside the convent.

No sooner had he checked into his hotel and reached his room than the telephone rang and the Bell Captain announced that the Mother Superior would like to see him. She exerted all of her charms upon him with the effect that he gave her a cheque for $2,000, which in those days was a substantial sum, and she went away seemingly very happy.

The following morning with his breakfast tray of iced water and orange juice Henry Ford had a copy of the local paper and on opening it was horrified to see the front page, announcing in very large letters that 'Henry Ford arrives in Town and donates $20,000 to the Convent'. No sooner had he read these headlines than the Bell Captain telephoned to announce the arrival of the Mother Superior. This time she was full of concern and said that she had already seen the Editor who had promised the following morning to publish an equally prominent headline to the effect that the gift was $2,000 rather than $20,000, UNLESS OF COURSE . . .

Henry Ford agreed to give the Mother Superior a cheque for a further $18,000, provided that he could dictate the inscription over the door to the new home, which, of course, was readily agreed.

In due time the Home was built and Henry was given the honour of performing the opening ceremony. A curtain was draped across the entrance and, pulling a cord, he exposed the inscription over the door, which read 'A STRANGER, I CAME AMONGST YOU AND YOU TOOK ME IN'.

*   *   *

One of the members of my staff, a known churchgoer, arrived on a Monday morning some three weeks ago with a black eye. On being questioned by his colleagues as to how he sustained the injury he told them that the previous day at Matins he sat behind a girl wearing a silk dress. When she stood up for the first hymn the silk, as it is wont to do, clung to the back of her legs and her thighs, riding up in an undignified way. Noticing this he helpfully pulled it down for her but she, apparently misunderstanding his motive, rewarded him with a black eye.

The following Monday morning he arrived with the other eye blacked. When his colleagues said, 'Surely you did not pull that girl's skirt down again' and he replied, 'No, I didn't, it was the man next to me, but knowing that she didn't like it I tucked it up again for her.'

His Honour Judge Aron Owen
Ph.D.
A Circuit Judge

Moses descends from Mount Sinai and addresses the waiting Israelites.

'I've got good news and bad news for you. I'll give you the good news first.

The good news: I've got Him down to Ten.

Now the bad news: Adultery is in'.

*   *   *

Judge, to a member of the Jury Panel who was about to be sworn in but who stated he was deaf in one ear:

'I'm afraid you can't serve on the Jury. You can only hear one side.'

*   *   *

A very nervous young policeman was giving evidence in the Magistrates' Court about the arrest of the defendant in the dock charged with alleged behaviour causing a breach of the peace.

Policeman: 'He was using bad language to me when I arrested him.'

Magistrate: 'What did he say?'

Policeman: 'He called me "a worship", you bastard.'

Sir Peter Parker

M.V.O.

Politician

Printing errors can be such a joy – and I found this one relevant too in the mergerous '60's when takeover bids were at their highest. With the United Nations booklet about the problems of housing in some parts of the Philippines, I recall, and in describing details of some of the environment living conditions there in the villages, it was explained that the real problem was the rush-mating on the floor.

*   *   *

When the professionals in management became too dogmatic about how much they can measure in successful enterprise, I always think of that incident on the M1. A lorry driver was driving along and pretty well once every mile he stopped the lorry, leapt out of the cab, ran alongside the lorry and banged it with both hands. Then he leapt back into the cab and off again. This strange behaviour soon caught the eye of our ever vigilant police, who followed him.

Sure enough, this kept happening: out of the cab, bang the side of the lorry and off again. Finally, the police car stopped and asked the driver what he thought he was doing. 'Oh,' he said, 'this is a two-ton lorry and I am carrying three tons of budgerigars. I have to keep one ton in the air at any one time.' The good manager knows there is one ton in the air in any organisation – not all his problems perch on the branches of the organisation-tree.

John F. Phillips

C.B.E., Q.C.

President, Private Patients' Plan, Founder Master of
The Worshipful Company of Arbitrators, 1982-1983

One story that has always had a rather special appeal for
me relates to the case of the rather complacent
businessman who, having delivered an after-dinner
speech at an important public occasion, turned to his
neighbour (who happened to be Oscar Wilde) and said to
him, 'now tell me; how would you have given that
speech?' Oscar is said to have replied, 'I think perhaps
under an assumed name.'

*   *   *

One device employed by after-dinner speakers who have
to propose the health of the guests or of some group of
people is to devise a noun of assembly or collective noun
to describe them. One of the best of such collective nouns
that I have heard was produced at a conference of
Vice-Chancellors and Principles of universities, held at
Delhi, when the speaker described the present company
as 'a lakh of principles'.

His Honour Judge Pigot

Q.C.

Common Serjeant, City of London

The Truth, The Whole Truth and Nothing But the Truth
But –

A wealthy American industrialist who was not an
emigrant from Ireland, wished to discover his family's
origins. He believed that he was descended if not from
one of the Pilgrim Fathers or the Pilgrim Mothers at least
from one of the Daughters of The American Revolution.
He hired a genealogist. The only ancestor traced was the
grandfather and he having been convicted of murder had
been sent to death in an electric chair. Such information
would have displeased the industrialist and this
displeasure would have been rewarded with a low fee.

Consequently he duly reported to the industrialist that,
with difficulty, he had been able to trace his grandfather
who had occupied a chair in applied electricity in one of
the foremost male institutions and had died in harness.

Lady Porter

Ex-leader of Westminster City Council
Deputy Chairman, London Festival Ballet

An American got married and said to his wife that she could do anything she liked in the house except for one thing and that was she must never look in the top right-hand drawer of his desk.

For 27 years they were married and she never looked in his desk drawer.

One day she was spring cleaning and could not resist the temptation of looking in his desk drawer. In it she found three golf balls and $5,000.

When her husband came home she had to confess that she had looked in the drawer and could not understand why she had not been allowed to look in there before, because there were only three golf balls and $5,000

The husband replied and said that he had to be honest and admit that when they got married he decided that if he played hookey he would put a golf ball in the drawer.

The wife said, 'well in that case it was only three times in 27 years and that is quite alright. What about the $5,000?'

'Well', the husband replied, 'I have to say that every time I got a dozen golf balls I sold them.'

*　　　*　　　*

A man of 82 called to see his Doctor to ask for a check-up to see if he was fit enough to get married again.

The Doctor examined him and said that he was absolutely fine and that he could see no reason why he should not get married again. 'How old is the new bride?'

'22', the man replied.

The Doctor said it was absolutely fine to get married and asked if he had a large home. 'Yes, quite big', the man replied.

The man got married and about six months later when walking in the park saw the Doctor. The Doctor asked how his marriage was. The man replied, 'it is absolutely fine and in actual fact I am pleased to say that my wife is pregnant'.

'By the way', the Doctor asked, 'did you take my advice and get a lodger?'

'Yes, as a matter of fact I did', the man replied, 'and she is pregnant as well!'

Dr. J. M. Rae

M.A. Ph.D.

Past Headmaster, Westminster School, Writer and
Columnist

Two after dinner stories that I have always liked are
these. The Headmaster was ill in bed on the day of a
Governing Body meeting. At the end of the day the
Secretary to the Governing Body came round to see him
with the following message. 'The Governing Body wishes
you a speedy return to health. This Resolution was
passed by nine votes to eight. With five abstentions!'

*   *   *

Herbert Fisher, who was Lloyd George's President of the
Board of Education in the First World War, was asked
after the War to speak of his experience to the Academie
Française. Having been educated at an English public
school his mastery of a modern foreign language was
small and he did not realise that the word 'Cabinet'
meant something quite different in French. He started his
address with the immortal words *'Quand j'etais dans le
Cabinet sous Lloyd George.'*

His Honour Judge Ranking
Judge of the Major's and City of London Court

A tale of the late Lord Atkin, I believe. He was the fifth speaker after a dinner, and had to reply on behalf of the guests.

The hour was very late, he said: 'Ladies and Gentlemen, it is very late. I have two after-dinner speeches – a long one and a short one. I propose to give both: the short one is "Thank you"; the long one is 'Thank you very much".' He then sat down.

Frederic Raphael
Author

There was a legendary Hollywood screenwriter and socialite called Charlie Lederer. He belonged to the group that used to hang out at the Hearsts' place and he had a good deal of experience of elegant living. During the war, his easy manner and good connections were put to diplomatic use. He was sent on a mission to India and on one occasion is said to have attended a reception at the house of a very snobbish English lady who was particularly proud her collection of Ming china, which was displayed in a delicate Edwardian case. This lady asked Lederer how he liked India. 'Fine,' he replied. 'Of course,' she told him, 'it's not what it was, socially. Nothing has been the same since the war.' 'It seems OK to me,' Lederer said, 'what's wrong with it?' 'Well,' said the lady, 'for one thing, the place is thick with Jews.'

Charlie Lederer was fair and handsome and tall and he was, I think, only half Jewish, but it was a half he refused to dishonour.

'Don't you like Jews then?' he asked. 'Oh, I don't think anyone does, do they?' his hostess said. 'And for what reason don't you like them?' 'Well,' she said, 'I don't know that I've got a *reason*.'

Charlie Lederer was a rich man and he had a lot of nerve. He reached up to the bobble on the very top of the Edwardian cabinet with the priceless Ming china in it and, with a single gesture, he flung the whole thing down onto the marble floor before his appalled and astounded hostess. He pointed a teasing finger at her and said, 'Now you've got a reason!'

*   *   *

The Garrick Club does not often honour its members with dinners to celebrate their eightieth birthdays. It did it for Dickens, I believe, and it did it for Willie Maugham. Now

Maugham, like many of us, detested giving speeches. He had better reason than most because he had a fearful stammer, which he controlled, most of the time, but never conquered. However, he was a man of punctilious courtesy and when his health was proposed, he had to respond. He managed well with his opening words, in which he thanked the clubmen for their generosity. He then declared that his health was not bad, considering, and that although he regretted the passing of youth – he knew it had finally gone, he said, when a young lady sat in what he called the *'strapontin'* seat in a taxi cab, leaving it to him, the Old Party, to join the other elderly persons in the comfort of the upholstered part – and wished that he could again enjoy the pleasures no longer available to him, nevertheless being eighty had its compensations.

At this point, his stammer appeared to have locked into permanent silence. He stood there without saying a stuttered syllable. The members waited, and they waited, and they waited, and they waited. A pause could be covered by the blowing of a nose or the sipping of a drink, but the pause lengthened into something almost unendurable. Willie would have to be rescued in a moment or two, wouldn't he? Willie finally rescued himself. He looked balefully at the sympathetic company and he said, calmly, 'I'm just trying to remember what they are.'

Artful as ever, he had used his known defect as a means of procuring suspense and, as he must have known, the thunderous applause which relief and admiration supplied.

Sir Lindsay Ring

C.B.E., D.S.c., D.Litt.
Lord Mayor of London, 1975

When asked to make a speech it is sometimes advisable to discover how long one is expected to 'bang on' for. I once asked my host the question. 'About five minutes would he adequate', he replied. 'With this sort of audience it's a little difficult to know where to begin', I remarked. He said he thought the fourth minute would be ideal.

*   *   *

Some ten minutes after take-off on a trans-atlantic flight a passenger in the 'No Smoking' area felt in need of a cigarette. The air hostess assured him there were several vacant seats in the smoking area further back and he soon found himself next to a cheerful Irishman. He apologised for disturbing him, at which the Irishman welcomed him heartily and added . . . 'and have you just got on now?'

*   *   *

The vital statistics of a mermaid:
    36 : 24 : and 75 pence a pound.

The Rt. Hon. Lord Robens

P.C.

Industrialist

Medical Professor: 'What would you do in the case of a person eating poisonous mushrooms?'
Student: 'Recommend a change of diet.'

*　　　*　　　*

'I can't sleep' wailed a voice in his ear, as the doctor got out of bed at three in the morning and answered the telephone.
'Hold the line' said the doctor crustily, 'I'll sing you a lullaby.'

Robert Robinson

Writer and Broadcaster

Yvonne Arnaud and Gladys Cooper were appearing together in the provinces. During rehearsals, Miss Arnaud stepped out into the garden adjoining the theatre and found Miss Cooper already stretched out on the grass. 'Doesn't that mean rain?' Miss Arnaud enquired sweetly of no one in particular.

Jean Rook

Columnist

Did you hear the one about the young reporter who was sent to cover a volcanic eruption, and was told by his News Editor, 'We don't want purple passages and fancy stuff like Jean Rook writes. All we want is the facts, the facts, the facts'.

The young reporter found out what time the volcano erupted, how many people were killed and how many people were injured. The facts, the facts, the facts. He then went and overlooked the scene and his whole soul – every journalist has one – rose inside him and he wrote a terrific purple passage which began, 'As the mighty, flaming, gushing volcano subsided, God sat upon the mountain above this little village . . '

He got an immediate telegrams back from the News Editor, '. . . Scrap the facts, interview God'.

Alderman David Rowe-Ham
Sheriff of the City of London, 1984-1985

Another Railway Carriage Story!

In a compartment of three people two very proud fathers were talking about their sons and one said to the other, 'My son has only just turned 35 and already he is destined to be head of his chambers and appointed one of the youngest recorders ever', to which the other replied, 'That's nothing, my son is aged 25, is a qualified barrister and shortly off to the Hague on a case of international repute'. There was a pause and the third man in the compartment could not contain himself any longer and with a sense of real pride looked up and said, 'That's nothing at all, my son is aged 16 and already he is helping the police with their enquiries'.

G. W. Rowley
F.I.P.M
Town Clerk of the Corporation of London

A man went through life bearing a guilty secret that his father had been hanged for murder. He concealed it from everybody until he applied for life cover. The proposal form required him to state the age of his parents when they had died, and the cause of their death. After much thought he replied that his mother had died at the age of 79 from a heart attack and that his father had died at the age of 40, and the cause of death was that he was attending an official function when the platform gave way.

Norman Royce

F.R.I.B.A., P.P.C.I.Arb.

Past Master of the Worshipful Company of Arbitrators,
President of The City Livery Club

At the end of the last war, Tiger Force was formed for the
long range bombing of Japan. Squadrons were trained in
readiness but the atom bomb was dropped and the
Squadrons flew only on sorties and not operationally.

Some aircraft were lost and one pilot was shot down and
badly burned. Fortunately he was rescued and flown to an
Australian base hospital where he underwent surgery. It
was a poignant scene in the operating theatre when he came
out of the anesthetic. He felt terrible. Slowly his eyes focused
and he saw an attractive Australian nurse bending over him.
He murmured to her, 'Did I come here to die?'

She gave him a lovely smile and in her beautifully
cultured Australian accent answered –

'No, you came here yest-a-die'.

*   *   *

A 17-year-old Italian immigrant boy was very worried, he
had become very fond of two sisters, Maria and Theresa
and could not make up his mind which one to choose
before approaching their father, so he went to seek the
advice of his priest.

He said, 'Father, I love them both but I do not know
which one to choose, please help me.'

So the priest said, 'My son, all you have to do is go into
the church and pray for guidance and the answer will be
given.' So he entered the church, knelt down and prayed.
After a while he looked up and was delighted to see the
sun shining on him through the window.

He rose, rushed out and shouted, 'Father you were
right. I prayed and suddenly the sun shone through the
stained glass window and there was the answer for me. I
looked up and read the words: 'Ave Maria'.

Sir Percy Rugg

D.L.

Chairman of G.L.C., 1967-1968

THOUGHTS ON AFTER DINNER SPEAKING

Usually it all begins by someone inviting you to be a guest at a dinner and then lower down in the letter are some such words as 'Would you please say a few words after dinner?'

When did this habit of after dinner speaking begin? Lord Birkett once suggested that it began with the woman in the Bible who, finding the lost piece of silver, called all her friends and neighbours together and said 'Come, rejoice with me.' History does not relate whether that was the only speech made on that occasion but it certainly gets full marks for the correct length.

*   *   *

A certain distinguished Society were very anxious to have a certain professor come and give their Society a lecture but every time they invited him he declined, saying that he could not accept because Monsieur Rubiloff was playing that evening. After this had gone on for some time the Society noticed that Monsieur Rubiloff was playing in their home town on a certain day so they sent off another invitation to the professor asking him to come on that day to speak to their Society. They received the following reply:

'I am afraid I cannot accept your kind invitation to address your Society. I note that Monsieur Rubiloff is playing in your town that evening but I am not interested as to where Monsieur Rubiloff is playing. I am only interested in *when* he is playing because when Monsieur Rubiloff is playing I spend the time with Madame Rubiloff.'

When the American Bar Association held its Meeting in London the Chairman of the Court of the University of London gave a small private dinner to the Chief Justice of the United States and other leading legal personalities. Towards the end of the dinner the Chairman leaned across the table and said to the Chief Justice Warren: 'There will be no speeches but I will present the toast to the American Bar Association in a sentence and you can acknowledge it in the same way.' The Chief Justice replied: 'That suits me very well for I have always remembered the saying that "A whale is in no danger of being harpooned except when he comes up to the surface to spout".'

*   *   *

The length of a speech is of vital importance. Mr Roosevelt was once asked how long he took to prepare his speeches. His reply indicated that if he were to speak for half an hour he would want two or three days; if for five minutes he would want a week; but if he had to speak for two hours he could begin straight away.

*   *   *

Hospitality is the art of making your guests feel at home when you wish they were.

*   *   *

Bernard Shaw, on returning home from a party one evening, was asked by his wife whether he had enjoyed himself. He replied: 'Of course I did my dear. There was nothing else to enjoy.'

Sheila Scott

O.B.E.

Aviator, Lecturer, Actress, Writer

A man may kiss his wife goodbye.
A rose may kiss his butterfly.
Ruby lips may kiss the glass.
And you my friends . . . Farewell
 – Or it could be ended with Happy Birthday, or
whatever.

Sir Harry Secombe

C.B.E.

Actor, Comedian and Singer

Although the waiter service this evening has been
excellent, I have often on these occasions been reminded
about the Head Waiter who died and had engraved on
his tombstone 'At Last God Caught His Eye'.

The Rt. Hon. The Earl of Selkirk
K.T., G.C.M.G., G.B.E., P.C.

The difference between a diplomat and a lady is – if the diplomat says 'Perhaps', he means 'No', or he is not a good diplomat.

If a lady says 'Perhaps', she means 'Yes', or she is not a lady.

'Someone in the City'

A businessman on a visit abroad sent a postcard back to his wife which read:

'The weather is here. Wish you were lovely.'

His Honour Judge John Slack

T.D., B.A., LL.B., LL.M.

Judge and Author

A True Story

An Irish defendant appeared at the Crown Court indicted on four counts of burglary. He was politely insistent that he did not wish to avail himself of Legal Aid, preferring to represent himself. The Recorder who tried him explained in simple terms to the Defendant the various stages in the trial procedure.

'Thank you, Sir,' said Paddy, employing the then correct mode of address.

As the trial proceeded into the second day, a succession of witnesses called by the Prosecution had made Paddy's chances of acquittal appear remote.

Not slow to appreciate this, Paddy began addressing the Recorder as 'Your Worship'. After the luncheon adjournment the Recorder had become 'Your Honour'.

At the close of the Crown case, the Recorder explained to the Defendant his options. Thank you my Lord', said Paddy, 'I'll give evidence from the witness box'.

After the jury returned with verdicts of guilty on all counts, the Defendant's numerous previous convictions were read to the Court.

'Is there anything you wish to say in mitigation?' asked the Recorder.

'Your Majesty has been most helpful', said Paddy.

Colonel, Alderman Grevill Spratt

T.D.

Sheriff of the City of London, 1984-1985

Chairman of the Magistrates Bench in admonishing yet
again the perpetual drunk – 'You must spend all your
money on drink.'

'No, your honour,' was the reply, 'mainly on the fines.'

Oliver Sunderland

Master of The Worshipful Company of Carmen,
1985-1986

On the wall of a Maternity Hospital a large warning
notice was posted by a rather stern Matron for the
guidance of Nurses reading:
  'REMEMBER THE FIRST FIVE MINUTES OF A
HUMAN BEING'S LIFE ARE THE MOST DANGEROUS'
  Some wag had added in equally bold print:
  'THE LAST FIVE ARE PRETTY DODGY TOO!'

Jimmy Tarbuck

O.B.E.
Comedian, Television Star and keen golfer

The Secretary of an extremely upper-class golf club
arrived at his clubhouse one morning to find a tramp
asleep in the doorway. The old guy was smelling strongly
of drink, his hair was matted, his eyes bloodshot. His
clothes were a mess. Around him on the ground were
empty bottles, mute testimony to his night's work. A
tired dog lay asleep at his feet. His overcoats, of which
there were several, lay partly on him, partly around him
as a make-shift bed. Cold tea lay in a Billy-can. A
half-eaten sandwich was curling at the edges. Flies
attended it. A week's growth of beard demanded not so
much a blade as perhaps cutting shears. He was, in short,
a mess.

The Secretary, fearful of arriving golfers, nudged the
old tramp awake. 'Disgraceful' he thundered through a
clenched moustache. 'What the hell do you think you're
doing here? This is private property, a private club, I
demand you leave these premises at once.'

With calm dignity the tramp rose. He shook and
collected his clothing, arranged his beard and wakened
his sleeping brute. He moved slowly away from the Club
Secretary, then turned and froze him with a glare. 'This is
no way' he said, 'to attract new members.'

His Honour Judge Anthony Tibber

A Recorder of the Crown Court, 1976

A grandfather was discussing the Bible with his grandson.

'Were you in the ark?' asked the grandson.

'No', laughed grandfather.

'Then why weren't you drowned?'

The Rt. Hon. Viscount Tonypandy

P.C.

Speaker of the House of Commons, 1976-1983

At a funeral in South Wales an aunt of the deceased person tripped at the graveside and broke her ankle. When the local newspaper gave an account of the funeral it referred to the incident and said: 'This accident cast a gloom over the whole proceedings.'

Sir Alan Traill

G.B.E., M.A.

Lord Mayor of London, 1984-1985

To tell the truth I have a sneaking admiration for Noah,
for he had the initiative to float his company when the
rest of the world was in liquidation.

The Rt. Hon. Lord Tweedsmuir
C.B.E., C.D., L.L.D. (Hons.)

Two men went fishing together in a lake. For a time they caught nothing. Then, suddenly, they found that the boat was surrounded by a shoal of fish. They caught all that they wanted and then fell to discuss how they could find this marvellous spot on future expeditions. The first man said that he would dive overboard and paint a circle on the bottom of the boat. The other agreed that this was a splendid idea and they rowed back to the Landing Stage feeling very contented. It was only when they got there that the second fisherman raised a doubt. 'Suppose', he said, 'we don't get the same boat next time?'

Terry Waite
Author and Broadcaster

I accompanied the Archbishop of Canterbury on an official visit to Nigeria, where Anglicans across the country displayed remarkable enthusiasm. Their enthusiasm was not matched by their command of English, as one street vendor had painted across the top of baseball caps which he was selling: 'Welcome to the "Holly" Father'.

The Archbishop and his Chaplain were further startled to discover another street salesman selling balloons stamped with the Archbishop's picture. His sales line was: 'Support the Anglican Communion and blow up the Archbishop of Canterbury!'

Ian Wallace

C.B.E., Hon. R.A.M., Hon. R.C.M.

Singer, Actor and Broadcaster

An American holidaying in Scotland goes into a small country inn. The only other customer is a wiry little man in a tweed cap with a Collie asleep at his feet.

'Excuse me', says the American, 'Are you a farmer?'

'Aye'.

'What size is your farm?'

'Oh, just a wee farm – mebbe ten acres.'

'Ten acres! Do you know, friend, back in Texas I can get up at sunrise, saddle my horse and ride all day 'till the sun goes down and d'ye know in that time I'll only have covered a third of my farm!'

'Aye', replied the farmer. 'I had a horse like that once!'

Irving Wallace
Author

ON CENSORSHIP

The most persuasive arguments against censorship, at least to my mind, are the following:

There must be certain laws in a civilized society, but any laws that dictate what a citizen can say or not say, read or not read, are dangerous. They can only escalate, until some people are telling other people what they may worship, how they may vote, how they should live. As my hero, Barrett, says in *The Seven Minutes*:

'If you can make me believe in a little pregnant, you can make me believe in a little censorship. And even a little censorship, I suspect, were such a thing possible, might be too much, far too much, because of what it could lead to. George Bernard Shaw spelled it out. Assassination, he said, is the extreme form of censorshp. And it is, and I'm not forgetting that.'

Another argument against censorship is – who is there to find the all-wise, all-purpose censor to tell us what we can or cannot read or speak? As Juvenal once stated – who is to stand guard over the guards themselves? Something that may be obscene to you may not be obscene to me. Or, as my hero, Barrett, put it in *The Seven Minutes*:

'Can anyone dictate tastes, when tastes and taboos differ so? They differ from state to state of this Union, and in every country of this world. One is reminded of Sir Richard Burton's story about a group of Englishmen who went to visit a Moslem sultan in the desert. As the party of Englishmen watched, the Moslem's wife tumbled off her camel. In doing so, her dress slipped up and her private parts were revealed to all. Was the Sultan embarrassed? On the contrary, he was pleased – because his wife had kept her face covered during her accident.'

Perfect.

The Rev. Basil Watson

O.B.E., M.A., R.N.
Vicar of St. Lawrence Jewry-Next-Guildhall

On godly children

The family hamster died. Christopher, its five-year-old
owner, wished to give it a decent burial in the garden. He
rallied his young friends and conducted a service. From
the kitchen window his mother heard him despatch the
hamster: 'In the name of the Father, and of the Son, and
into the hole he goes.'

*　　　*　　　*

On Orchestration

Dr Ralph Vaughan Williams' tune to the hymn *For all the
Saints* is a great favourite of mine. His name plate
alongside the door of his house in Wimpole Street caught
the eye of a girl from the Welsh valleys who had come up
to London looking, so she hoped, for medical help from a
fellow countryman for the trouble into which she had got
herself. Her ring at the bell met with a brusque reply from
the housekeeper: without an appointment she could not
possible see the Doctor. So she dejectedly walked down
the street not really believing that the doctor was so busy
that he could not see her. She retraced her steps, but for a
second time got the rough side of the housekeeper's
tongue. 'But I didn't expect to see him,' she said, 'merely
to find out what made him so busy tht he cannot see a
poor Welsh girl who is in such trouble.'

'If you really want to know,' replied the housekeeper,
'I'll tell you.'

'Oh thank you, please do.'

'Well, I will: he's orchestrating the Men of Harlech.'

'Just my luck,' opined the hapless girl, 'if only he'd
done it three months ago I would not be in my present
trouble!'

Katharine Whitehorn
Columnist and Author

An old Russian peasant is walking along in the icy evening and as he comes towards his home a little bird falls out of the air, frozen stiff by the icy wind. He picks it up, musing that there is nothing that he can do for it and throws it on to the warm dung heap beside his door, then goes in to sleep on his stove as Russian peasants do.

But the bird actually is not dead, it is merely frozen stiff; the warmth of the dung heap revives it and it sits up to sing a paean of joy at still being alive; whereupon a passing fox hears the song, comes over and gobbles it up.

Moral: he that puts you in it is not necessarily your enemy; he that gets you out of it is not necessarily your friend; and if you *do* find yourself in it don't make too much of a song about it.

*　　　*　　　*

Aaron, who couldn't sleep at night, was tossing and turning, and finally his wife said, 'Aaron, what is it, I can't bear it any longer, something must be worrying you, you can tell me what it is.' So eventually, in the middle of the night, he says, 'Well, I've been trying to keep it from you Miriam, but now I'll tell you: The terrible thing is, that I owe my friend Moishe money. I owe him £500, I can't pay it, I don't know where I can get the money from and I can't sleep at nights for worrying about it. What can I do?' His wife thinks for a few minutes and says, 'Aaron, I can't bear to have you worrying so much and unable to sleep at night. I will tell you what to do. You will tell your friend Moishe that you can't pay him the money. And then you can let *him* worry.'

The Lord Wigoder
Q.C.
A Recorder of The Crown Court
Liberal Chief Whip, House of Lords, 1977-1984

An old boy of 91 got engaged to an 18-year-old blonde. He went to his G.P. for a check-up before the wedding. The G.P. warned him of the dangers of the excitement that lay ahead, and added that the consequences might be fatal.

'Well,' said the patient, 'if she dies, she dies.'

Dorian Williams
O.B.E.
Broadcaster and Author

A nun ran out of petrol driving in Wales on a Sunday. She walked a mile to a garage but it was closed. The proprietor's wife said she knew that her husband kept a one-gallon container; she could have the gallon, but her husband would never let her part with the one-gallon container. What could it be carried in? Then she remembered an old-fashioned chamber pot that she kept upstairs. Would that do? Of course. So the nun set off to her stranded car carrying the gallon of petrol in the chamber pot.

She was just pouring it into the car's tank when a huge lorry stopped. The driver poked his head out of the window and said: 'Madam, I am afraid that I cannot share your religion – but my God, I admire your faith!'

Emlyn Williams

C.B.E., M.A., F.R.S.L.
Actor and Playwright

At a dinner lately, I sat next to a very chic older woman who seemed vague about most things; one could guess that she lacked concentration except on such subjects as valuable commodities on sale in Bond Street and thereabouts. Our not-very-original conversation turned to 'mugging'.

'Oh', she said, 'last week the most awful thing happened to a woman friend of mine – not strictly mugging, worse really, so sinister . . . She was walking down her street, feeling so happy in a mink coat her husband had just given her for her birthday, when a handsome man walking towards her stopped, smiled warmly and said, "My dear, what a beautiful coat!"'

'"Oh, thank you," said my friend, imagining the man knew her, "I'm so glad you like it . . ." "Oh, but I do," he said, still the warm smile, "may I have it please?"'

She looked around, and when she realised that there was not a soul near them, she nearly fainted. "Take it off," he said, still with the smile. She was petrified, and slid the coat off. He took it, bowed, walked slowly away, disappeared round the corner, never to be seen again. Can you believe it?'

I was of course fascinated by the story – she was right, it was particularly sinister. 'What a dreadful thing', I said, 'with nobody about, to be robbed like that – I imagine it was dark?' 'Oh yes, that's what made it so awful for her – beautifully dark, the very best mink . . .'

Sir Max Williams

President of The Law Society, 1982-83

Two minor poets died and when they arrived at the Gates there was St. Peter to greet them. Sorry! said St. Peter, but I only have room for one minor poet and so we'll have a competition to decide which of you should come in and I will take the one who has the better poem ending with the word 'Timbucktu'.

The first minor poet started:

> 'As I stood on desert sands
> Gazing over the shimmering lands
> The caravaner hoved into view
> On his way to Timbuktu'

The second minor poet felt he could meet the challenge and said;

> 'Tim and I a hunting went
> Spied 3 maidens in a tent
> As they were 3 and we were 2
> I bucked one and Timbuktu'

Lord Willis of Chislehurst
F.R.T.S., F.R.S.A.
Playwright and Author

At a retirement dinner:

'Today we honour a man who doesn't know the meaning of the word dissemble, who doesn't know the meaning of the word fear, who doesn't know the meaning of the word surrender. And so, we have all chipped in to get him this dictionary.'

*   *   *

Prison authorities in Oklahoma forgot to execute double murderer James White, and yesterday he was granted a reprieve. White, 24, who has appealed against execution, said: 'I remembered but I wasn't going to say anything.'

Sir Hugh Wontner

G.B.E., C.V.O.

Lord Mayor of London 1973

A visitor to a London Hotel was ordering his breakfast. He said he wanted two boiled eggs, one so hard it was like a bullet and the other scarcely cooked at all; he wanted three pieces of toast, absolutely black on one side and not toasted at all on the other; and some cold coffee.

'Oh, sir, we can't do that', said the astonished waiter.

'Why not?', said the visitor, 'You did it yesterday.'